A 1 COMPLETE

dagg

CW00954332

A COMPLETE dagg

JOHN CLARKE

With illustrations by Jenny Coopes

A Susan Haynes book

Allen & Unwin Australia

Sydney Wellington London Boston

First published in 1989
Third impression 1989
A Susan Haynes book
Allen & Unwin Australia Pty Ltd
An Unwin Hyman Company
8 Napier Street, North Sydney, NSW 2060, Australia

Allen & Unwin New Zealand Limited
75 Ghuznee Street, Wellington, New Zealand

Unwin Hyman Limited
15-17 Broadwick Street, London W1V 1FD, England

Unwin Hyman Inc.
8 Winchester Place, Winchester, Mass 01890, USA

National Library of Australia
Cataloguing-in-publication

   Clarke, John, 1948-
     A complete dagg.

   ISBN 0 04 360071 9.

   1. Australian wit and humor. 2. Australia—Politics and government—1976-
   Humor. I. Coopes, Jenny. II. Title.

A828'.302

Set in 11½pt Highland by Midland Typesetters, Maryborough 3465
Printed by Australian Print Group, Maryborough, Vic.

CONTENTS

WATCH THIS CHAP

by Barry Humphries

John Clarke was born in New Zealand, resides in a beautiful district outside Melbourne, and was once 'axed' by the Australian Broadcasting Commission. He is Australia's best humourist.

In the early 1970s he lived for a while in London and played a minute role in *The Adventures of Barry McKenzie*, a comic film of mine about an innocent abroad who drank out of tins and never took off his hat—a formula which, I am happy to say, has ensured the popularity of subsequent Australian movies.

During the screening of 'rushes' the director, Bruce Beresford, slowed down the film. It was an ingenuous scene of carousing Australians bidding goodbye to the hero. One of the actors wearing a sleepy and impassive expression continued to drain his glass merely raising an index finger in peremptory farewell. Beresford froze the frame. *Watch this chap*, he said. It was John Clarke.

Mr Clarke is still an actor preferring to perform his own material, although he has written for other comedians and on rare occasions the screen credits have said so. His style is dry, deadpan, laconic, seemingly improvised to conceal the careful artistry of the writing. Like that other great Oceanian artist Michael Leunig he is crudely and shamelessly plagiarised.

It is no easy task to satirise Australian life. A society which can accept, for instance, the elevation of Mr Bill Hayden to the office of Governor-General—albeit with a howl of resigned derision—is a society with a formidably high satire threshold. It might indeed be said Australia satirises itself, bypassing the professional.

There is a transcendental humbug, even an endearing grossness about Australian political life which has imbued every man, woman and child with a profound and sardonic cynicism. The Judiciary, the Civil Service, the Government and the Media have inspired sixteen and a half million DIY Voltaires and Dean Swifts.

John Clarke sees the skeletons in our closets, and I am amazed he has not grown very rich on offshore hush money. In Australia the Powers that Be are very powerful indeed and are protected by draconian laws of libel that would make an Australian *Private Eye* unthinkable. The press bullies, hoods and monomaniacs who hold, or have recently held, high office demand critical immunity.

Fortunately for John Clarke he can always be dismissed by his victims as a harmless wag, an amusing ratbag and an anodyne parodist. If he told us what he sees and what he knows about Australian society in any other but his jester's guise he would, long ago, have met with a very nasty accident.

He is an isolated and courageous figure, who has analysed and dissected contemporary Australian life with a precision absent from the work of his more slapdash, politically bigoted contemporaries. The interviews with a Prime Minister and a Queensland Demagogue are models of their kind; hilarious, subversive and beautifully written. In fact, some of the material in this book which is transcribed from wireless broadcasts reads as well as it sounds.

Like all artists fired by some divine indignation he has a few bees in his bonnet: the fatuity of sport (*viz* golf and farnarkeling), the interminably repeated sitcoms which infest Australian television, the absurdities of officialdom (nourished by his ABC experiences), the deification of the adman and, above all, the grotesque dichotomy of a country stridently boasting of its freedom yet supporting a gigantic and bureaucratic incubus.

Yet Clarke's art, for he is an artist, make no mistake, is to show us our national follies without animus. He is also revealed in this book as a gifted parodist, and the political encounters in the manner of Damon Runyon are particularly brilliant. If there were—impossible thought—an Australian *New Yorker*, Clarke would be its luminary.

We should be grateful to have between the covers of one book such a rich selection from the Dagg archive, a book which is impossible to read without a fixed smile. We should also be grateful that the remote land which gave the world David Low, the kiwi fruit, Katherine Mansfield and the hot air hand drier also gave us John Clarke.

FRED DAGG

AUSTRALIA: A USER'S GUIDE

In which it is revealed that
minor problems exist within the
framework of Australian
society. Many helpful hints are
provided.

In response to questions from confused members of the Australian public, many of whom are known to me personally, I've embarked on a programme of national education.

Too little is written about the ignorance of the Australian people. There is, by way of contrast, too much written about their intelligence. Their resourcefulness, initiative and fearless traditions have been set to music in order to sell a wide range of foreign products; the Anzac spirit is evoked by no one more beautifully than American fast food chains, and the chairman of Australian Steel has been made a Sacred Treasure by the government of Japan.

The problem of educating the Australian population is clearly urgent and must be addressed on a scale never before contemplated. We've started at a very rudimentary level with a massive television campaign designed to teach people what a Post Office is. We've tried to do several things at once, which is a sophisticated concept, but one we like. We're explaining:

(a) What a Post Office is.
(b) Who those people are, in Post Office uniforms, who deliver your mail.
(c) What those things are, that are put in your letter box (through a slot in many cases) by the uniformed artisans mentioned in (b).
(d) What those boxes are. (The ones in which articles are placed by the liveried representatives of the essential service industry alluded to in (a).)
(e) That when it's raining, the mail is delivered in the rain.
(f) That during periods of intense sunshine, the mail is not delivered in the rain.
(g) That in order to effect delivery, some postal employees use bicycles, although on very steep hills, particularly when the mail is not being delivered in the rain, the bicycle may choose not to be ridden but to be pushed.

We've referred to the Post Office throughout as 'Australia Post', a catchy name meaning Post Office. In fact, we've been even cleverer than this would imply. We've decided to improve our logo. Initially, I wasn't sure this was possible. The old logo has been extremely successful and, despite claims that it was unnecessary and meaningless, research has demonstrated that many people realised eventually that the logo had something to do with Australia Post, which, of course, they associated with the Post Office. Aside from these practical considerations, the logo is very appealing to the eye and is a fine example of Australian design at its triumphant best.

There is no limit to the amount of money we're prepared to spend on developing a new logo. The cost is simply not a factor. The stakes are too high for petty mercantile considerations to be of any significance. What we'd like to do is annihilate our competition so comprehensively that it will be almost as if it hadn't existed.

I know this all sounds new, but we've done something very like it before. We ran a visually very satisfying campaign some time ago explaining to people what a telephone is. (In effect, a telephone is a thing that rings in the mountains of southern Europe, and the ringing stops if you pick it up and cry into it.) It worked better than we dared hope, and at the time of writing there is now only one organisation operating nationally as a provider of telephone services.

In some countries, of course, both Telecom and the Post Office would be owned by the state, and the millions spent on advertising would be wasted on improving services and lowering costs.

So buoyant did we feel after all of the above, and such was the feeling around the office, that we decided to keep going. Gamblers will know what I mean when I say we felt we were 'on a roll'. It was resolved on a show of hands that we adopt the suggestion made by the young work-experience person, and change the name of TAA. We tinkered briefly with the conceptual work and decided to call it either 'Australian Airlines' or 'Australia Post'. We eliminated 'Telecom' because we wanted to avoid imagery of mountains and crying and making expensive telephone calls to women who live alone in Surrey. After a heated lunch we also ruled out 'Australia Post' because despite the many common elements (uniforms, rain and sunshine), aeroplane travel and group cycling are fundamentally different. We felt this difference demanded expression. Very few of the sample group associated the name 'Australian Airlines' with the Post Office, and TAA is, as everybody has known for years, an Australian Airline. Simple really; 'Australian Airlines'.

But how to sell it, how to market this intricate and yet muscular idea. The answer was, of course again, Educate the People. Paint all the aircraft, order new badges, new paper, new hats, new buildings, new front doors for the vans (the cost of all this to be charged against 'Improvements'.) Follow this with a massive multi-media campaign, trumpeting the arrival of a completely new airline that no one has ever heard of, and which only a small number of people will think of as the Post Office.

I have seen criticism of our decisions, but it is petty and ill-informed. I will not dignify it with a response.

I don't mean to harp on about this, but there still isn't anything like enough public money being syphoned into the advertising industry. There are plenty of government-owned bodies spending virtually nothing on nebulous ideas and anthem quality statements of the obvious.

I exclude the Post Office from this. I know I've been critical of them in the past, but my hat is now raised in a gesture of respect. Their television commercials have made them the market leader right across the country.

They have filletted the competition to the point where, I believe I am right in saying, in some areas the Post Office is now the only Post Office still operating as a Post Office.

I also have only the highest regard for the millions sensibly invested by Telecom in establishing that a telephone can be used for making phone calls. I may have oversimplified this. The commercials actually indicate that a telephone can be used for making overseas or interstate phone calls. There is no suggestion that it is possible to make local calls, but there is probably a reason for this. Perhaps the phone is out of order and no one can look at it before Wednesday, or maybe all the phones in the whole area are out and nobody knows why, or it is possible that the phone has been cut off because the user is too poor to go on helping with the TV commercials.

Neither do I intend any disrespect to the airline that used to be TAA. Their work in establishing whatever their new name is has been without parallel in the history of image-based money-flushing, although they didn't have it all their own way. The Buy Australia Campaign must have given them an awful fright.

This was a bench-mark effort. It pointed out that people should not buy Australian products just because they were Australian. This broke down the old, stereotyped idea that a commercial should achieve what it set out to do. The Buy Australia Campaign depended for its success on the ability of the buying public to reject the advice of its advertising. I'm presuming here that the aim of the campaign was to encourage people to buy Australian products, supposing such a thing were possible.

It would be unfair to ignore also the spectacular media-spending embarked upon in the name of the Priority One Campaign. It would not be at all appropriate to remember the campaign itself, but the figures involved were very reassuring.

For the Bicentennial one can have only the most open-hearted admiration. Not only are they currently funding about a quarter of the world's shipping, but the plan to sail the Deficit around Australia during the summer months is well advanced and the television campaign is on air, even though it obviously isn't quite finished yet. There is a song about all of us doing something without hands. I'm sure it will all become clear once it has been edited.

It is what is called an 'awareness' campaign. It doesn't sell anything or provide any actual information. Its main aim is to be on television. It can then be demonstrated that a number of people might have watched it. They will be 'aware' of it.

Whether or not the Bicentennial can recover from this advantage remains to be seen. There can be little doubt, however, that so far they are doing everything expected of them.

What I want to know is, where are the other government departments? Where are the awareness campaigns for the Weather Bureau and the Official Receiver? Should their Australian-ness not be celebrated?

Would not the romance of Soil Erosion lend itself to the screen? It is Australian Soil Erosion, after all. It is the best bloody Soil Erosion in the world and it wants to tell its story. A more natural subject for a song would be difficult to imagine. It has everything; wind, rain, floods, the pitiless heat of the sun. Perhaps the Weather Bureau could be part of it. The Official Receiver should also be approached without delay.

There are others of course. The Albury-Wodonga Development Corporation, for instance. Isn't this the sort of dream that sustained the lads in trenches all over France and Belgium? Is there an Australian heart that does not quicken at the mention of The Inspector of Inflammable Liquids or the Department of Lifts and Cranes?

These people cannot be expected to continue unless their work is accorded the simple dignity of being described within an inch of its life and sung about by groups of white Australians who are not hanging from prison ceilings.

A BOLD FUTURE FOR BROADCASTING

There seems to be some opposition to this business of amalgamating the ABC and SBS. Good grief. Let me explain.

We have been wondering what to do with the ABC. We've had various studies done, and a series of commissions have been established over the years to look into the performance of one another, and it has all come to a head recently because of a need to rationalise the operation in line with current policy.

The short list of suggestions at the planning meeting was predictably impressive.

1. Change the name of the ABC to Australian Airlines and run a series of commercials, costing whatever, depicting a large group of uniformed employees becoming very excited about being filmed being very excited. Possibly with a rousing air punching anthem and plenty of booming drums.

2. Change its name to Australia Post and run a lot of expensive commercials showing the capacity for things to be done during weather.

3. Amalgamate the ABC with Telecom and commission a string of increasingly perceptive commercials establishing that millions of dollars worth of glossy advertising will make management feel better. (This has yet to be established, but I'm pretty sure something of the sort must be the case.)

4. Designate the ABC as the official mouthpiece of the Buy Australian campaign. Advantage: we wouldn't have to give a great deal of public money away to a small group who control the communications industry. Disadvantage: we wouldn't be able to give a great deal of public money away to a small group who control the communications industry.

5. Sell the ABC to the highest bidder, bearing in mind that there are no bidders. The ABC has only one thing worth buying: its audience. The question is not how to privatise the ABC, where the news now consists almost entirely of promotions for stories yet to come, and well-woven thank-yous between news people and sports people and weather people and frequent announcements by reporters of their names and where they are and sometimes even the date and the fact that they are appearing on ABC news, which is not as surprising to the audience as you might expect. There is obviously little time left for news, and it's hardly surprising there isn't any. They've also employed someone to talk over the credits of the programs

in a voice that makes three syllables of 'and', the way they do on commercial television, which many people don't like, which is why the ABC's audience exists.

A substantial part of this audience has already gone to SBS, certainly for news and current affairs and such things as entertainment. If we amalgamate them while simultaneously destroying the ABC's already reduced capacity to deliver to what remains of its own audience, we'll force the audience either to commercial television or away from television altogether, thereby privatising that audience.

There remains ABC Radio, which is the best known example of the relationship between the smell of an oily rag and the will to keep going. They hide in the hills, these people, and they come down at night, destroying railway lines and making off with army property. We know who they are. We have names.

We remain, of course, deeply committed to the maintenance of the very highest standards in broadcasting in Australia, and we salute ABC management in this regard.

I don't want to seem to be over-reacting here, but there have been a number of unfortunate remarks made about the very sensible decision by some of the people in the banking dodge to institute charges for cheques. Personally I can't see that it's anyone else's business what banks charge their customers, in fact I'm surprised that they have gone to the trouble of telling their customers the new arrangements are about to be introduced.

The charges are completely justified and more or less essential. Banks provide services to their customers, and some of the customers, not all, but some of them, have been abusing the system by using the services. They open a cheque account for instance, and then sit down and write a whole lot of cheques.

Now this sort of thing is not on. A cheque account is supposed to be a convenience, by all means, but not for the customer. Let's look at the facts. A cheque account is opened and a range of charges come into effect straight away, the meter is running from the kickoff, and no matter how much money is in the account, the bank never pays any interest unless the customer puts the money in a different account, where it can't be got at so easily, and if the account is overdrawn the bank charges interest as well as the charges and it charges charges to charge the interest, which is only fair.

They don't always trouble the customer with a formal announcement of this, they just do a little takeaway sum down the right hand side and put the money in another account marked 'whoopee'.

If money is deposited from another account held by the customer, the interest-bearing total in that account decreases, obviously, and the bank charges a fee for transferring the money, which again is fair enough when you consider the amount of work involved. On top of which, of course, the bank then safeguards the customer's money. Particularly, as it happens, from the customer. If the customer goes into the local bank where the staff consists almost entirely of members of the customer's immediate family, small amounts of money can be obtained by standing in a queue among video machines depicting holidays in places the customer can't afford to go.

If the customer turns up at another branch of the bank and writes a cheque, the bank safeguards the customer's money by assuming that the customer is someone else who has stolen the customer's cheque-book and the customer's accreditation from the bank, identification, driver's licence and credit cards, and frequently some of the customer's children, and is on some kind of rampage with the customer's very limited funding.

Of course if someone comes *in* with some money, and looks like an identikit photograph and wants the money deposited in fifteen different names and if there are any problems, ring this number and ask for the tooth fairy, that's obviously OK.

Perhaps the romance of Banking does not weave its happy spell over every heart, and I fully understand that my own case may be unusual.

I ran away from home at the age of nine in order to go into merchant banking and I was fortunate enough to secure a position as a deck-hand with one of the bigger operators. As the name might imply, my job was mainly in the service and backup area. If people didn't pay on time, I used to deck them with my hand.

In time, of course, I went into International Money Management. I was given an eye-patch and a parrot and was told to put in for water some time near the end of June.

I don't intend to chronicle my entire career here, but Banking has a human side and I often find that a personal anecdote can break down a prejudice and open the mind of a bigoted person.

People must understand that the plight of Australian Banks at the moment is one which concerns us all. I won't go into too much chapter and verse on the history of this because frankly we still don't know quite how it happened, but somehow the Banks have found themselves providing a service to their customers. The position could not be more serious.

The problem is a thing called Bankcard. We introduced it a few years ago in order to encourage people to get into debt so we could charge them interest on money we knew they didn't have.

We nominated a date by which the money we knew they didn't have had to be paid back, and when it wasn't, we reluctantly hopped into them for the going rate.

We advertised it as a convenience, which of course it was, since we were able to do all this without even leaving the building. The retailers took to the idea immediately.

The old convention of selling goods only to those who can

afford to pay for them had long hampered the retail trade, but now they could sell to anyone and they began laying in stocks of anything at all in a full range of colours.

The right to insult the customer was retained by the practice of checking each Bankcard against a secret list of axe-murderers provided by Interpol and kept somewhere under the counter.

It was all going fairly well and Bankers all over the country were fighting to keep a straight face when suddenly the appalling truth became apparent. Many individuals were actually paying their Bankcard accounts when they received them. People were, in effect, paying the card off as they used it.

In other words, the only return to the Bank was from all the customers' other accounts, from loans, mortgages, leasing arrangements, property speculation, overdrafts, service fees, duties, levies, general adjustments and whatever alterations to interest rates seemed like a good idea at the time.

Compensation and restitution must be paid to banks immediately if the economy is to remain upright. Freeloading and other forms of deception must stop. The public has selfishly and wilfully abused a very noble experiment and the proposed $30 charge for Bankcard will not go close to covering the damage.

The following initiatives must be introduced if the Banking industry is to survive.
• A $40 fee charged to people who don't have a Bankcard. This is only fair.
• A handling fee of $5 on all transactions of any type at any bank during banking hours.
• Bank officials to be authorised to wear balaclavas and to cosh likely prospects in the street at a rate not exceeding 150 an hour.
• The reintroduction of deck-hands.

It is only through improvements of this kind that Australian society's present values can be maintained.

I was greatly saddened to see that the Australian Share Market walked into a lift-shaft the other night as it was on its way back to the party with more of the Chateau La Fite and another tray of larks' uvulas. Just in case this happens again before we get the area roped off, there are one or two little rules of thumb which might help if you're not quite sure what's going on.

Firstly, if ever a Government tells you that it is letting market forces determine the character and value of the media sector, stand well back and pull the collar of your coat right up high. If you're not careful the owners of media will borrow heavily in order to take each other over, charge the interest bill to the taxpayer and the Government will be left as the sole investor in the amount that is wiped off the value of the shares. The media owners themselves will be all right. They probably won't pay much in the way of tax in the short term because they've taken a very slight shower but they've got enough money to go about the battlefield rolling the bodies over and picking up anything shiny.

Secondly, if ABC Television, which is owned by the Government, is going to bring us the news and call it the 'Crash of '87' because everyone else does, and put a graph up behind the newsreader showing a great big line which starts high up on the left hand side and goes down towards the right hand side, and if the attitude is to be one of astonishment about how on earth it all happened, make sure they haven't been running a separate section inside their own News programme every night whipping up excitement about the geniuses who are making a quick buck in the stock market.

And make sure the experts they wheel on to discuss the graph are not stockbrokers or market analysts. And if they're Treasurers who've deregulated the money market, make sure someone asks some questions other than 'What's your favourite colour', and 'Did you lose a fair bit yourself?'

Because if the indicators that the economy was in such marvellous condition last week are the same indicators that are now being described as having nothing to do with the economy, then I think we should get the Fire Brigade in and see if they can't smell burning.

If the economy is sufficiently sound as to be impervious to

all these fluctuations in the paper value of guesswork, then why is it being constantly pointed out how seriously this will affect everybody? If this isn't cleared up the 14 million Australians who don't own shares might just have an election one of these Saturdays and come up with a Government to look after their interests.

There is a great deal of publicity being given at the moment to an outfit called The New Right. This is because the Old Right (who tend to own such trinkets as radio and television stations, magazines, newspapers and other items covered by the Not Nailed Down legislation) have decided to stimulate debate in order to keep the Government on its toes while the trapdoor is oiled and the shadow cabinet is fitted into a landing-craft.

I was a foundation member of the New Right and have been involved in the development of much of the New Right philosophy. I reluctantly left the movement in late August following an internal wrangle over the colour of the tunic and the insignia on the hat. However disappointed I might have been by what was, for me, a watering down of our original aims, I nevertheless still share many of the ideas and aspirations I see being broadcast through our official outlets.

That said, I note with mounting concern an apparently wilful failure in some quarters to fully understand what we are saying. I blame education for this, and I'll tell you something for nothing; when we get in again, the loonies in the teacher unions will hit the ground running. I heard a schoolteacher the other day on a radio program about children (for Christ's sake) saying that every school anywhere in Australia should be able to provide a good standard of education. To which my response is 'No thank you very much, indeed. Begging your pardon, but we don't live in Russia (pause) not yet!' I digress, I'm sorry, but education was one of my areas of responsibility, and I won't abide cant.

In essence, the philosophies of the New Right are based on a recognition of the value of the individual and an abhorrence of anything that stands in the way of the individual, such as unions, bureaucracies, taxation, regulation or other individuals.

I can perhaps best illustrate this by example. We favour the introduction of university fees, although I forget why, because obviously only the wealthier type of individual will be in attendance. We oppose land rights on some very sound basis that just eludes me for the moment, and we favour uranium exports to France because of a wide range of factors. We favour the idea of people working for the dole because it provides a sense of dignity for the people for whom the people on the dole are working, and it gives the unemployed an opportunity to work without contributing to anything approaching a wages explosion. There is absolutely no need for a Commission for the Future because we favour uranium exports to France, and we question the alleged 'right' of single mothers to benefits from the state. If we start giving way to one group, pretty soon we'll have the taxpayers' money being used to help bloody near anyone who needs help! This defeats the very purpose of taxation, which is to find ways of reducing taxation.

I might say, while I've got you all here, that these views are not simply those of a small group outside the mainstream of Australian politics. The Liberal Party contains many of our leading lights, the Labor Government is implementing some of our more imaginative suggestions and although I appreciate that many people find it necessary to deplore us loudly at dinner parties, I think we are all sufficiently grown up to know what's really going on, and I hope as many of you as possible can make it to the barbecue on the 15th.

CONTRACEPTIVE-VENDING MACHINES BANNED IN QUEENSLAND, SAYS PREMIER

Brisbane, Thursday.

At a time when the United States has a peacekeeping force in the Gulf in order to incite the Iranians to attack, so that the war can break out on a decent-sized scale while they're up there in order to make sure it doesn't happen, and Bob Hawke has responded to the call for a treaty with the Aboriginal people by saying it's out of the question although he's deeply committed to the idea of something a bit like it and he's prepared to stand on one leg for the six o'clock news, it is a source of great comfort to many of us to see the Queensland Government's courageous decision to make its citizens safe from precautionary measures.

There has been criticism of this initiative, certainly there has, although it's fair to say the vast bulk of it has been rather childish and predictable knee-jerk rhetoric which takes no particular account of the obvious benefits of recent events in the region.

The fact that the Police are being trained to break into public lavatories is not something I think we should dwell on. Admittedly it may be seen as a slight disadvantage but only in the very short term and with any luck the novelty will wear off before it becomes a social problem.

The reason that contraceptive-vending machines are being crowbarred from walls and taken away for fairly detailed questioning is that they promote promiscuity. This is quite well understood and I don't want to go into a lot of detail, I think we all know the feeling. Who among us has looked at a contraceptive-vending machine without experiencing a clanging of the hormones and a tendency to approach people in the street with a range of unnatural suggestions.

There isn't a more overtly erotic image anywhere in the world than the prospect of a contraceptive-vending machine. Even photographs of contraceptive-vending machines can do the trick on occasions and many a jaded marriage has been given a new lease of life by the parties getting together and engaging in a full and frank exchange of views on the subject of contraceptive-vending machines.

As with any sound argument, of course, this thesis can be tested by the consideration of its opposite. What do people do if they do not have access to contraceptive-vending machines? And again, the answer is obvious. They don't experience any sexual desire. It simply never occurs to them.

It's not the condoms that are the problem. I realise the Premier indicated at one stage that they were, but he's been under a lot of pressure for a number of years and if we were all held responsible for the things we say on national television, we'd be in a fine old mess, both as a nation and as a people.

If the condoms were the trouble they wouldn't be freely available in chemists and supermarkets all over the state. The problem only exists where people are buying them in order to put them into vending-machines. It's OK if people are using them to prevent sexually transmitted diseases. That's what they're for. That's obviously all right. In fact I understand the cause of the trouble has now been identified and the Queensland Government condition can be expected to improve.

Reykjavik, Friday.

What can I tell you about this majestic country? As the plane banked and began its descent a few short days ago, I was immediately struck by the vastness and apparent emptiness of the landscape. Much of it is covered in ice, of course, which conspires with the pale northern sky to obscure the horizon and give the impression of endless light playing on an invisible screen.

The land itself seems by contrast much darker than it probably is, and the wildflowers look vibrant, almost as if they are on fire. I was a little fatigued by the long flight (having been routed from London through Copenhagen and Oslo for security reasons), and when I had checked in to the hotel and taken a brief pounding from room service, I slept until 10.30 the following morning.

After breakfast I strolled around the central part of Reykjavik, which is a very attractive town and is steeped in history. There is much to catch the eye and the traveller is afforded a decidedly pleasant hour or so, just wandering and letting the interesting sights and the memorable people leave their indelible mark. More than a third of Iceland's population of about 250,000 lives in Reykjavik. It is not difficult to see why.

I had an excellent cup of coffee at a little restaurant whose roof was shaped like a viking helmet and where, I was told, Bobby Fischer used to buy cakes on his way back to the hotel. (The currency here, incidentally, is the krona.)

I fell into conversation over coffee with the European correspondent from the *Baltimore Sun*, a Ugandan photographer working for UPI out of Paris, and an East German radio reporter who spoke immaculate English and who had me on a bit about working in a country where a handful of people control all the newspapers and all the radio and all the television. I explained things as well as I could, but his unfortunate proficiency in English prevented us from reaching a point of genuine understanding.

He was a rowing buff, and he insisted on paying for my coffee on that basis, Australia apparently being well regarded in that field. (The currency here is the krona, by the way.)

The Museum is a lovely old building, and the displays themselves are superbly laid out. I didn't have time to do justice to the place, actually. I could easily have spent the whole day in there. Of course, the influence on Iceland of other cultures such as Norway, is considerable. It is perhaps at its most considerable in the case of Denmark, which ruled the 40,500 square mile island until fairly recent times. Despite this, Iceland has the oldest parliament in the world, the Althing, which was founded in 930. The people of Iceland have long been a seafaring people, and their contribution both to navigation and fishing is universally recognised. The wide acceptance of fish generally owes much to this courageous race. For anyone wishing to know more about the early history of the region, I recommend the Icelandic sagas, which tell of the Vikings and are famous throughout literature for so doing.

On the Tuesday, a few of us (a BBC cameraman, with a brother in Adelaide oddly enough, an American Strategic Arms commentator, and a diplomatic correspondent for the *Glasgow Evening News*) chartered a small plane and went on a slightly hairy but very absorbing flight around some of the northern coastline. There's also a great deal of volcanic activity on the island, and in the afternoon I took what I hope will be a very good photograph of the *Chicago Tribune's* man in Scandinavia with steam coming out of his hat.

The hotel does a range of fish dishes, and the greater part of the evening was spent wrestling with various chowders and different manifestations of the genus cod. We had a few drinks of some rather deadly local fire-water, and after a session around the piano we ebbed away to our beds in preparation for the long flight out the following day.

I hope this has been of some interest to you. I actually went up there to cover the Disarmament Talks between the United States and Soviet leaders, but I can't cheat that story much beyond a paragraph.

Gorbachev listed the things he was prepared to concede, the missiles he was prepared to dismantle, the numbers he was prepared to reduce, and a five-year plan for doing it. Reagan said he wasn't prepared to concede anything, wasn't aware the talks were about disarmament, hadn't been briefed and had a fair sort of idea Gorbachev was a Russian.

Do try to get to Iceland if you can. The currency is the krona, from memory.

As has been extensively reported in the mainstream press, complicated legal action has been undertaken by the British Government to attempt to prevent the publication of my book *Catcher in the Spy*. The book is essentially a chronicle of events as they were perceived and experienced by me during the period of my involvement with the British Secret Service.

I should perhaps say that the British Secret Service is not a secret service in the sense that its existence is a secret. In point of fact, its existence is quite well known. The secret is the extent to which it is the Russian Secret Service.

The Australian Government, pausing briefly in its important work of closing down alcoholic rehabilitation centres for Aboriginal people, this week considered its position as owner/manager of a secret service begun and developed by the area sales manager for at least one and possibly two other secret services. Hence the trouble over publication.

The legal argument was essentially this: if a book is written about things that are secret, the things won't be secret any more. Books about the secret service cannot therefore be published if they are written by people who know about the secret service. This not only protects the secrets themselves (which although known to the British and probably known to the Russians and the Americans, are at least still secret from the public) but also brings books about the secret service into line with books generally.

While all this was going on, however, I reached a very satisfactory arrangement with the proprietors of a large format wine journal, and we decided that regardless of the outcome of the trial, extracts of the book would be published. The public, which is so often kept completely in the dark, the public which after all pays for the secret service and is now footing the bill for the legal battle, deserves a fair go. The right to knowledge is surely fundamental.

I would emphasise that much of the book is based on actual diary entries, which were often made under trying circumstances. It is a personal memoir. It is recorded in good faith, exactly as I recall the incidents described, and I apologise to anyone whose name I may have left out.

'In late August of 1949 I was detailed to travel to an address in South London. I was to give my name as Arnold Watkins.

I was given a history of Watkins to study on the way down; artillery man, North Africa mostly, MC, couple of languages, that sort of thing. Upon arrival at what looked like a furniture store, I was met by someone who introduced herself as Mary but whom I knew as Squadron Leader Harry Jackson. He whistled a pre-arranged sequence of notes, and I followed him up what I now realise was a flight of stairs. He revealed to me that in a room at the rear of the Georgian building's second floor there was at that precise moment a meeting of the top KGB agents operating in Western Europe. They had sent out for coffee, and I was to take it in. "We want names," I was told. "We want faces, anything that's said or done, photograph it with your eye."

'A waiter entered the building at street level and was coshed expertly and stripped by practised hands. Within minutes I had donned his livery and was entering a large room carrying a tray of steaming cups.

'At the head of the table sat a man called Boris Ivanov who had been in Vienna on the afternoon of May 11 but who hadn't been seen since and who was known to be number three in Moscow. Next to him was a rotund fellow in the Russian manner, smoking a cigar and grunting impatiently from time to time. I wanted to hear his voice, but he said very little and was difficult to understand. He had a strange way with the letter S, which like many of his countrymen he converted into a sort of click by trapping it in one cheek and squashing it into something more like a ch. When importuned as to his need for sugar with his coffee, he denied me a verbal response by rather rudely holding up two fingers. He doodled on the back of an envelope with a fountain pen. The pen had no initials engraved upon it nor any manufacturer's name. His idle drawings gave no clues to his identity and seemed to be nothing more than rows of bricks stacked on top of one another.

'Directly opposite him was a young woman with a lovely smile. She had an airline bag which barked occasionally and into which she placed a number of gingernuts as the business of the meeting was conducted. She wore a crown.'

To be continued . . . Copyright, *Catcher In The Spy*, 1986.

My first contact with Australians was in London, where I was living during the early 1970s for tax purposes. At one stage, seeking a career in retailing, I wrapped mail orders in the back of the book department of Harrods. Each volume was placed on a piece of corrugated cardboard and the cardboard was then manipulated until the book was no longer visible. A skill I have never lost.

Across the bench from me was an Australian who called everyone Bruce. He pointed out a friend of his in the sports department. 'See him Bruce?' he said. 'He's a professional tennis player.'

'What's he doing working in the sports department of Harrods if he's a professional tennis player?' I asked.

'He's no good,' said the Australian.

I lasted three days at Harrods, but my Australian friend lacked my persistence and was impeached on the second afternoon for putting a famous sign on the main stairs. It was made of corrugated cardboard and said: HARRODS, NO FARTING.

It was at this point that I recognised the shared perspective of Australia and New Zealand on matters of international significance. The question is whether or not this communion of subversives can be converted into export dollars.

Closer Economic Relations will do much for the exchange of ideas among business people of course, although it should be remembered that there is really only one idea among business people and exchanging it is an achievement of only modest dimensions. It must surely be possible to develop something more worthwhile than the intercourse of moustachioed primates in Flag Inns all over both countries.

A new nation should obviously be forged, combining the two in such a way as to maximise the contribution of each. Australia would grow fine wools, beef and trees for Rupert's newspapers. New Zealand can provide dairy products, coarse wools and trees for Rupert's other newspapers. Bob Hawke should head a government, possibly in Brisbane where there hasn't been one for a while and where it will have novelty value.

Roger Douglas is an automatic selection as Minister for Finance. Someone would have to explain the job to him, but once he understood it he'd be hard to hold. He is dedicated to excellence in all things and is apparently a delightful person.

His appointment would also eliminate the need for the portfolios of Health, Education, Social Welfare, Housing, Agriculture and the Arts.

Paul Keating is the best Treasurer in the world and could run an expanded banana republic with his eyes closed. Indeed that might be where he's going wrong at the moment. New Zealanders will have to get used to the idea that the Stock Market Crash was 'a correction' and that it confirmed the brilliance of Paul's mid- to long-term thrust, but this shouldn't be a problem. The correction was almost terminal in Wellington and drove at least one correctee to camp in a Sydney living room with twenty-seven journalists and a change of tennis socks.

David Lange would be Speaker. He has been trying to curb this tendency lately but there seems little point and a man who only shaves because it provides him with an audience has much to offer an emerging nation. If the post of Governor-General is available I would suggest almost anyone except Alan Jones or Kylie Minogue and I submit the following changes to the governmental structure of all states in the new federation.

The bicameral system obliges the government of the day to deal with vestiges of the last government but three. The same thing happens when cousins marry and quite clearly there should be one House, as is the case in New Zealand, with the proviso that the power should be retained by the states, as is the case in Australia. This will allow for spirited debate and important pronouncements which have nothing to do with the running of the country and will accommodate both the New Zealand yearning for regional independence and the Australian desire for a perpetual Constitutional crisis.

The new Parliament House in Canberra can then be turned into an all-weather sporting complex, thereby satisfying the only genuine interest of the entire population of both countries.

HAWKE RETAINS TITLE

Lakes Course, July.

The West Australian Bob Hawke played steady golf here last week to carry off the prestigious Canberra Open and ensure for himself a place in history and a small fortune in endorsements and commercial affiliations, some of which were announced while the tournament was still in progress.

His game was not spectacular at any stage, but neither did he falter under pressure. He maintained his rhythm beautifully and took no silly risks in returning a final-round 71, consisting of eighteen straight pars and setting a standard for the rest of the field to beat.

He accepted his victory philosophically and spoke briefly of his humility before writhing uncontrollably and singing 'Happy Birthday' to his wife on national television during what would otherwise have been the presentation ceremony.

Equal second were Sydney rookie John Howard and the veteran Ian Sinclair, a couple of strokes clear of several well known names not including Bjelke-Petersen, the Queensland trick shot exponent who went to pieces in the conditions, and the Tasmanian clothes horse, Michael Hodgman, who missed the cut.

Weather was a big influence on proceedings here, with rain and wind on the second day playing havoc with reputations. Hodgman lost his ball at the first and again at the second, the fourth, the fifth, the sixth and the eighth. Hobart amateur Robin Gray found Hodgman's ball on the green at the difficult tenth and buried it in a sandtrap.

Hodgman asked for a ruling and was told to take a drop, although it was obvious to the gallery that he'd already been doing this for quite some time. It took him five shots to get out, and his approach shot looked fine until Gray stood his bag on it. Hodgman took a 13 and hasn't been sighted since.

The third day was even worse. Driving rain and very limited visibility greeted players at the first tee, and by 8.15 storm cones were hoisted and the course was practically unplayable. It was at this point that Bjelke-Petersen's championship hopes were seen off the premises.

Playing in snow shoes and a borrowed raincoat, he pulled out a 3 wood and drilled a good-looking tee shot into the mist.

Nobody knew exactly where the ball had gone, and there was some surprise when it reappeared over the roof of the clubhouse behind the tee and struck Petersen in the back of the neck while he was consulting a yardage chart. There have been suggestions recently that he should perhaps be playing on the Seniors' Tour, although according to officials he's too old.

Peacock was also out early and not at all impressed.

'It was appalling,' he said. 'I've never played in weather like it. It's extremely serious.'

His playing partner, Ian McPhee, pulled off some wonderful shots, including a 4 iron from up a tree in the light rough to eagle the seventh, and he finessed consecutive birdies at the eleventh, twelfth and thirteenth. He said later that although conditions were not ideal for the players, they were a great deal worse for the crowd, many of whom had no jobs or proper homes.

The only player with a genuine chance of catching Hawke on the final day was Howard, who shot a commendable 72 in the worst of the third round-weather and was three over for the tournament, although he announced at a press conference that he was 15 under according to figures available from Jim, his caddie.

The final round was played in dense fog, and it was sometimes difficult to know what was happening. At the turn Hawke's game was holding together nicely, and the Howard challenge couldn't seem to quite get going.

Howard's club selection was at times inexplicable. He had a number of birdie putts and for some reason after brief consultation with his coach, Jack Valder, he hit every one of them with a sand wedge. Anything close to the green he hit with a 2 iron and he drove at the par 5 fourteenth with a putter 'to keep the ball under the wind'. These costly errors had dropped him back to 5 over after 9 holes, despite Jim the caddie's claim that he was 29 under the card and had broken the course record.

Hawke's victory is an interesting one. He has completely rebuilt his swing in recent years. As a youngster he was a prodigious hitter of the ball but had a tendency to hook everything to the left, frequently leaving himself no shot to the green and sometimes finding himself with an impossible lie. But with application and an ability to copy the big money earners, he has developed a flatter swing and a more consistent short game.

The results speak for themselves and are largely responsible for increased corporate sponsorship and a falling off in public attendances.

Scores:

R J Hawke: 68. 69. 71. 71.

J Howard: 69. 76. 72. 93.

I Sinclair: 70. 75. 69. 95.

P Keating: 64. 63. 117. 88.

G Richardson: 98. 97. 96. 95.

R Rae: 97. 102. 78. 91.

A Peacock: 112. 78. 78. 112.

I McPhee: 63. 73. 83. 113.

J Elliot: 99. 104. 71. 68.

B Hayden: 63. 63. 64. 174.

G Evans: 68. 69. 91. 103.

G Hand: 71. 71. 71. 98.

R Willis: 68. 86. 87. 88.

M Hodgman, T Uren, B Cohen, C Hurford, A Geitzelt, G Scholes and L Bowen all missed the cut.

CELEBRITY INTERVIEWS

In which persons of significance
are engaged in light
conversation to good effect.

An interview with Robert James Lee Hawke, Prime Minister of Australia.

Mr Hawke.

Keep it brief son. I've got a fair bit to do.

I wonder if we could talk a little about the change in your political stance in the last five years.

What change?

Are you suggesting there hasn't been a change?

Look we're not going to get anywhere if you don't watch my lips. I simply asked 'What change?' I'm seeking further information as to the meaning and character of your inquiry. If I could think of a more elementary way of expressing it, believe me, you'd be the first to hear about it.

I appreciate your frankness.

Good. What change?

You were once a conservative.

Was I? That's interesting.

And you've become a kind of left-wing radical.

Just pop a flare up when you've finished.

Hundreds of thousands of Australians who used to support you now feel they've been tricked and that the country's just about stuffed.

Do you have a question or are we here for purely rhetorical purposes?

I have several questions.

Let's have them one at a time. I'm sure they're extremely searching. Each will require intricate consideration.

Why the change? What caused it?

Can I make a suggestion?

Yes.

Ask me if there's been a change in my political stance.

Has there been a change in your political stance?

No, there hasn't. There's a difference between being in opposition and being in government. People have got to realise that when they vote a party into office, the party will do what it promised to do. If that's different from the sort of thing that was done by the previous government it's not because the PM has changed his mind, it's because the country is now being governed by a different party.

But you said a Labor government would be exactly the same as the previous government.

When did I say that?

1983. 'Four Corners'. 'If elected a Labor government will be exactly the same as the previous government.'

That's very dishonest of you. You've only quoted half of what I said. Read the rest of it.

'Exactly the same' you said.

Read the rest of it. I won't continue the interview unless you read the rest of what I said.

'If elected a Labor government will be exactly the same as the previous government. Let the Status Quo be our talisman, accountancy our sword.'

Exactly.

But you haven't done it.

Bullshit.

What about giving the Aborigines all that land?

We had to do that. It was a promise made by the previous government.

You abolished the $250 fee levied on university students.

Of course we did. A university isn't a middle-class finishing-school, it's a provider of Tertiary Education. It's paid for out of Taxation and the economic equation will only work if the Education provided is available to the people who pay the Tax. And I would ask you to remember that the rich don't pay tax.

Some of them do.

They don't pay much.

Some of them pay hundreds of dollars.

They get relief in other areas. We frequently help with the financing of a monopoly for instance.

Is it true that you're going to double all welfare payments and benefits?

There is no plan at this time to double them, no.

To increase them significantly?

We have yet to finalise our thinking on this matter.

Can you give me a categorical assurance that welfare payments and benefits will not be significantly increased under your government?

I'm not in the business of making statements of that sort. If anything is decided, a suitable announcement will be made.

When?

At an appropriate time.

You've been accused by some opposition members of being a socialist. Are you a socialist?

It's not a word I'd use to describe myself, no.

But others could?

I can't help what other people call me.

Thank you.

Thank you, comrade.

John Howard, Leader of the Australian Liberal Party and Her Majesty's Opposition in the Australian Parliament.

Mr Howard, thank you for your time. You're a very busy man.

It's cool.

My friends aren't going to believe this.

You're very kind.

Do you get a lot of fan mail?

Rather a lot, yes. I try to reply to it all, but I'm afraid it's just not possible.

Are you here for long?

This is a private visit and is necessarily brief although I hope to come back when I have more time.

What have you been doing in the last couple of months?

I finished work on a film in the middle of January. It's essentially *Dante's Inferno* although it's been reworked somewhat by Woody Allen and he has co-directed it with Marguerita Von Trotta.

Goodness. Who's in it?

Meryl's doing Beatrice and I seem to be doing Dante. Jack Nicholson and Paul Newman operate an outfit called 'Stygian Ferry-Rides: Refund if not completely satisfied'. There are various Furies, of course: Robin Williams, Cyril Cusack, Victoria Wood, Alec Guinness, Klaus Maria Brandauer, Bill Irwin, Tracy Ullman, Gielgud, Catherine Deneuve, Kate Nelligan and so on.

Isn't Barbra Streisand doing something in it?

She probably sings a song, I don't know. It was shot in Senegal and that sort of thing would be done back in a studio.

Have you seen the picture?

Yes, it's very good. I was quite pleased, although I haven't seen it with an audience because I was racing to finish a final edit on the book.

The Amnesty book?

No, that was published in November. This one's a novel.

I haven't heard about that.

No, you wouldn't have. I wrote it in French and I'm translating it into Italian, German and Russian before I do it into English. I've got a bit behind, unfortunately. I took rather too long over the Spanish version and by the time I'd finished the Masai I was up a well-known tributary.

Good heavens.

I might say it's not over yet, either. I foolishly undertook to render it into Chinese and, of course, I speak only Mandarin. All I can do in Cantonese is conduct rudimentary discourse about train timetables and hope to hold my own if the conversation drifts towards Confucian philosophy. Otherwise I'm completely hopeless.

What will you do?

I shudder to think. Probably go up there and learn it.

Are you pleased with the novel?

I honestly don't know. I think I'm a bit close to it.

This is not called La Paupière, is it?

Yes.

The one everyone says is going to win the Booker?

It had better not. I've read the last three books that did.

Didn't a painting of yours sell recently?

Not that I know of.

Someone in New York?

Ah! I know what you mean! No it was a sculpture. The Metropolitan bought a piece, yes, a bronze, I think. Not a very marvellous one, if you ask me. It was a joke, I think. Bianca said she liked it and a lot of rich idiots fell over each other trying to get at it. It's disgusting and I don't really bother now. The last exhibition I had, the average price was $300,000 a piece. I mean really! It's grotesque. People are starving for Chrissake!

Didn't you later reveal that you hadn't actually done any of the pieces?

Yes. The buyers were furious and extremely embarrassed and obtained a court order suppressing their own names.

What did you do?

Bought a pile of newspaper space and published all their names and addresses.

Did they sue?

Yes, and I went on national television and revealed that I *had* made the pieces, so suddenly they had no case and had paid ludicrous amounts of money for sculptures they now hated.

Can we talk about medical research?

Bearing in mind that I haven't been in the lab more than half a dozen times in a month.

Is it true that you discovered a hormone that causes anger?

Not exactly, no. I'm lucky to be working with a very remarkable team of biochemists and geneticists. I'm pretty much the donkey of the group. I make a lot of coffee. What they've done is isolate a mathematically explicable relationship between the growth-rate of medullary tissue in the adrenal gland and the distance from Vienna at the time of conception.

What do you think of Australian politics?

Irrelevant. Government doesn't matter in Australia. The country is run by profiteers and carpetbaggers and the economy is manipulated by international capitalists. It's deckchair time.

You're not impressed?

The politicians themselves may be very concerned and caring people and they probably mean well. They are obviously just not up to it.

Tragic.

It is. It's tragic.

Mr Howard, thank you.

Thank you.

Interview with Sir Joh Bjelke-Petersen, Premier of Queensland for nearly twenty years.

Sir Joh, when was it you first realised that you could make other people laugh? Was it the old schoolyard thing?

Yes I suppose it was. It's a defensive thing. There's always the bully isn't there? You've got to do something about it and with me it was always just making the other kids laugh.

You had trouble with authority at school I think, didn't you?

Not initially, but I changed schools when I was about eleven and I lost all my old friends and had to make new ones, and there was a teacher who made every attempt to goad me into insurrection so I could be punished within the law. In fact if I'm on about anything, it's injustice.

Do you remember anything in particular that you did, in those days?

A fellow who is now a meat-wholesaler and I once put a big sack of flour in the school chapel's air-conditioning during the annual re-enactment of the Easter Passion. That was good.

If we can talk now about some of those very 'Joh' things, the mannerisms, the little bits of verbal business that everyone hears and just thinks straight away 'That's Joh'.

You're thinking particularly of the 'Goodness me's' and the 'Don't you worry about that's' and so on?

Exactly.

The apparent confusion?

Yes.

Some of that was there very early.

How early?

I think we're probably talking fresh out of school here. I noticed that a lot of people, just in their normal speech, are inclined to fumble about a bit and that by exaggerating, I was able to strike a chord. I didn't very often use a script in those days either, which is another thing. And it's quite handy to have all your ideas just pile up and crash into each other because

34

it gives you time to think, as well as, hopefully, with any real luck, getting a decent-sized laugh.

I know you've probably been asked this a thousand times before, but who are the other comics you most admire?

Oh, Joan Rivers.

She's great.

I mean, can we talk? The woman's fantastic. The first time I saw her; heart attack.

Yes.

Really. Literally. Off the bed on to the floor, rolling about, in a ball, need for air, the full catastrophe.

But not an influence as such.

No, I don't think so. Different style, different subject matter.

Who did influence you then?

Well, I think my parents. There was always a lot of laughter in our home and I think that's terribly terribly important. The Keystone Cops.

The chaos?

Yes the way a chase would just start up and people would be chasing, no reason, no nothing and there'd be haystacks with people's running legs sticking out of them. And I suppose to a great extent I've tried to do that with language.

It is often said that there is a fine line between comedy and tragedy. Do you believe that?

My word.

Are you the sad clown? The Commedia del'Arte clown?

Well, I think I'm a very Australian clown. I think I'm a VERY Australian clown. I'm not immune to life's bleaker side, obviously, but I don't think I'm consumed by it either. I frequently find, for instance, the things which worry people, a lot, a lot of the things which worry people very badly, I find very funny. Personally, I find them very VERY funny, and I wouldn't want that to sound as if I don't care.

35

I didn't take it in that sense.

Good.

Before we go, Sir Joh, you've made a lot of great humour in your time. You have a lot of great jokes. Which joke would you consider to be THE joke, of all ones you've performed?

That's a difficult question, just casting my mind back now, as we speak. There is great emotional pull for me, for the car that ran on water. I always thought that was very funny.

Yes.

Very very funny. But I suppose in terms purely of audience response, sheer laughter, which is the ultimate measure of this thing, when I ran for Prime Minister.

Yes that was always my favourite.

Thanks. Yes I thought that went pretty well. I thought it was pretty funny.

Why do you think it actually worked as well as it did?

Various factors. First of all, let me say that it had been done before. It wasn't an original idea, people had been . . .

But you brought something to it didn't you?

Well I like to think so. I had a lot of luck with the timing. For instance, for a start I announced I was running for Prime Minister when there wasn't an election on.

Yes.

Pretty funny. Pretty funny.

Yes it was.

Right from the kick-off, I mean that is pretty funny. Then, an election was called, and where was I?

Disneyland.

Disneyland. Pretty funny. Pretty funny. Pretty funny. You've got to say that's pretty funny. I had a lot of luck with the timing. It couldn't have been better for me. There I am running for Prime Minister when there's NO election and then there IS an election and I'm at Disneyland, being photographed with big-nosed people in the background and speaking of my personal . . . I mean it was pretty funny.

Couldn't believe your luck.

Couldn't believe my luck. On a plate. Literally on a plate.

Sir Joh, thank you very much for your time.

Thank you, you've been a wonderful audience.

Mr Hill, can I ask you, have you ever produced a television programme?

Not personally, no.

Ever produced a film?

Not as such, no.

Have you ever written a film or a TV show?

No I haven't.

Did you ever design a set?

Not a set, no.

Any costumes?

Not costumes specifically.

Are you a member of Actors' Equity?

Not at the moment.

What about directing? Have you ever directed a film?

Not yet, no.

How about editing?

I've never done any editing at all.

Mixing?

What exactly is mixing?

Did you ever work in make-up?

No.

Were you ever a grip?

A grip? No.

Gaffer?

Do. I don't, thanks.

Ever worked with computer graphics?

Ironically, no.

Overseas sales?

Never heard of them.

Have you ever production-managed?

Are you looking for a yes/no answer?

Yes.

No.

Have you ever been a lighting director or cameraman?

Which one?

Either.

No.

What about sound-recording?

What about it?

Have you ever done it?

Professionally?

Yes.

No.

Non-professionally.

Sound-recording?

Yes.

No.

Have you ever worked as a film or television critic?

Not in the sense of actually doing it, no.

What is your current occupation?

I am the Chief Executive of the Australian Broadcasting Corporation.

Meryl Streep. Film actor. Her career began on the New York stage but she quickly earned a reputation for strong character portrayal in such films as 'Kramer v Kramer' and 'The Seduction of Joe Tynan'. She mesmerised audiences in 'The Deer Hunter' and then followed 'Silkwood', 'Sophie's Choice', 'Out of Africa' and more recently the slightly less mesmerising 'Heartburn' and 'Ironweed'. Looks nervously out the window better than anyone else in film today. When the dramatic story of Lindy Chamberlain's ordeal became an international movie, there could be only one Lindy; Meryl.

Miss Streep, you're filming in Melbourne at the moment.

Yes, we are. We're in the studio here and then after that we're going to the . . . what, the Northern Territory is it?

Yes, that's right. The Northern Territory.

Yes, the Northern Territory. And I'm looking forward to that a lot. That'll be great.

What sort of research did you have to do to understand the character you're playing, which, of course, is Lindy Chamberlain?

Yes, well I read the book of course—'Evil Angels'—the Bryson book. I read that. I've read thousands, literally thousands of press clippings. Piles and piles of them. I can't tell you. I've watched videos of her being interviewed, Lindy Chamberlain being interviewed in press conferences, round about the time of the trial and then again after she was released. I've steeped myself in it basically.

You actually met Lindy Chamberlain?

Yes I have. Yes, actually I have. Remarkable woman. Very, very, very impressive. Highly intelligent. Short. Quite a lot shorter than I thought. I thought she'd be taller. A very remarkable woman I thought. Highly intelligent with a lovely sense of humour too, which was nice.

Have you had any trouble with the accent as such?

Well, I've done a lot of work on the general accent. The general sort of Australian accent. I'm well aware of certain things you people do here, for instance your language, with the way you speak.

You mean the flattening of the vowel sounds.

Yes, flattening; a thinning of the sound I think as much as anything else; and the lengthening. You've got a habit of lengthening some sounds. Like the 'i' sound for instance, and then sometimes the consonants are clipped quite noticeably. Just listening to you talk I can hear you doing it.

Is it a nasal sound?

It can be, but I don't think it always is. I find it very attractive I might say. But what I've tried to do is get as close as I can to that Australian sound, but without actually doing an impression of Lindy Chamberlain. The difficulty for me really, is that the Australian sound is actually very different from the way I speak naturally, and to that extent it has been quite different, yes.

Do you get immersed completely in a role when you take it on for a film?

I do sometimes, yes. I did with Karen Blixen for instance in 'Out of Africa'. I found her a very inspiring and admirable woman really. I liked her.

In what way?

Well, I liked her. I liked her in quite a personal way. I liked her a lot. I found her very likeable. I felt we were quite close in a way. The 'Sophie's Choice' woman for instance I don't think I could actually live a role like that. I think that was slightly different, in a way perhaps more cosmetic . . . I felt more organically involved in the Blixen woman.

Silkwood?

Karen Silkwood. I think there is something of me in that. Yes, that very, that youthful quality I think, that she had, prior to her death. The carefree attitude. I can recall something of that in my own life.

Not present so much in the later period perhaps?

In my later period?

No. Hers.

Oh hers. Oh no, absolutely not. Absolutely not.

41

Have you met a lot of Australians before arriving in Australia?

I have met a lot of Australians, yes, before arriving in Australia. Yes.

If I could turn to your hair for a moment. In the film, is it your hair that you're using?

This hair here?

Yes.

Yes, this is my hair. This is not my natural colour.

Oh, right.

It's been dyed black. You know my natural colour is . . . well, it's a sort of a . . . well see my eyebrows?

Yes.

That's my natural colour.

Right.

The colour of my eyebrows. It's been dyed. Very, very black and it's been done in the style in which Lindy Chamberlain . . . well in this case, used to wear her hair. She's changed a little now. But it's being done by the hair people in the way she used to do it, but again it is not an impression. This is not mimicry here. I mean, I am not trying to become Lindy Chamberlain. I am trying to, as it were, imbue myself with certain characteristics that I see in Lindy Chamberlain.

I see. Finally, Meryl, I do have to ask you this question. Have you formed an opinion as to who did it?

You've got to remember that this has been my life for the last 6 months, and I've hardly done anything else. I've buried myself in this. I've read so much that I think it would be remarkable if I came out of it without an attitude about who had done it, so yes, I suppose I do have in that sense a private view about who did it.

Well, I have to ask you the question. Who did it?

Fred Schepisi.

Prince Charles. Always a welcome guest at any time and a great favourite with the crowds, especially since his marriage to the Lady Diana Spencer. Dedicated worker for the Conservationist cause and for stronger regulation in urban development.

May I call you Charles?

No, I don't think that would be at all appropriate. Your Royal Highness.

Your Royal Highness?

I think that's the expression you're searching for.

Your Royal Highness, what are you doing in Australia?

What am I doing in Australia? A good question. I'm here very briefly, to hand over to the Bicentennial Authority an anchor from a replica of a scaled-down model of one of the original barges which originally carried provisions in Portsmouth, out to the tall ships, prior to their coming to Australia in the first place.

You used to go to school here, didn't you?

I did. I did. I did go to school for a period out here. Yes I did. Yes at . . . at . . . oh . . .

Timbertop.

Timbertop, absolutely, in . . .in . . .

In Geelong.

In Geelong. Geelong. Absolutely.

Do you have any fond memories of Geelong or Timbertop?

Oh, very fond memories of Geelong, and of Timbertops frankly. Very fond.

What do you remember about Timbertop?

Oh, I remember that it was . . . it was in . . . oh . . .

Geelong.

In Geelong. I remember that very clearly. And I remember Geelong quite well, because . . . I went to school there for a period.

And is your wife with you on this trip?

My wife?

Yes.

She what?

Is she with you?

With me? On this trip? No, actually at the moment, she's opening a fête in Norway and was unable to make the trip . . . very regrettably, because she is normally at my side and . . . oh I miss her . . . I miss her a great deal.

There's been a lot of unfortunate publicity about your marriage hasn't there? In the papers recently?

There has. Yes, and it's difficult you see. I suppose these people have to sell newspapers and go about their business and it is difficult sometimes to deal with that, but I suppose one should see it in that context — and we certainly try.

Yes. Is there any truth to any of the rumours or do you and your wife get on well?

Oh yes. Famously. Absolutely. Oh, we get on terribly well, terribly well. I spoke to her last night. Oh, yes, absolutely. We get on very well. We speak to each other quite often.

You go out to the desert quite a lot, don't you?

I do.

Yes. What do you do there?

I think. I think. I think.

That's all?

Yes, I think. I go out into the desert and I think.

And what do you do when you come back?

I normally stop thinking when I come away from the desert. I find it easiest to think in the desert.

People say that you are very funny.

I suppose I am. I wouldn't have thought I was particularly funny. The business of going into the desert is really just a private . . .

44

What I meant there was that you've got a great sense of humour.

Oh. Sense of humour. Absolutely. I'm a Goon nut. I'm an absolute Goon nut.

Really?

Absolutely.

Which of the Goon characters do you particularly like?

Oh, Eccles was always my favourite. Yes, absolutely. I used to do him.

I was going to ask you that.

I used to do him at school at . . . at . . .

At Timbertop.

At Timbertop, I used to do him down there in . . . oh . . .

In Geelong.

In Geelong. I used to do him down there — I used to do his voice and I can still do it.

Would you like to do it?

Well, normally one does this in the bathroom so you have to imagine the echo . . . Well, I'll give it a go. Um . . . fine, fine, fine, fine,

That's wonderful.

fine, fine, fine, fine,

That's wonderful.

fine, fine, fine, fine,

Excellent.

fine, fine, fine, fine, fine, fine,

You've obviously been doing that for a long time.

Well, yes, I've been doing it for years, you know, I used to, I could do fine, fine, fine all day.

And when did you start doing that?

Oh it was, ah, well I started doing it when I was a kid, I suppose, as a child, I think, as a child, as a child. Yes, I suppose before

I was even ten. I suppose when I was nine I started doing that. I suppose when I was nine.

Are you still holding your hands behind your back as much as you used to?

I do that a lot. As a matter of fact I was taught that. I was taught that.

By whom?

By my father. I think one's father has a lot to teach one. He has a great deal to teach one about I suppose life's great lessons. And for me one of them was just keep your hands behind your back.

Right. Finally, Your Highness, if I could ask you this. You would like to be King?

I think I probably will be King, and I'm looking forward to it in lots of ways. In lots of ways I'm looking forward to it. In other ways of course . . . one approaches a job like that with some foreboding, some foreboding. Going to the desert is going to be very difficult to fit in . . . and you can't do much Eccles when you're the King. You really can't. You can't stand around in the sort of place and the type of raiment that one is required to don, in that capacity, and do Eccles. You can't do that and expect the monarchy to keep going.

Thank you very much Your Royal Highness, for giving up your time.

Thank you very much.

FARNARKELING

In which serious Australian
sporting achievements are
celebrated.

Korea. Thursday.

The Australian Farnarkeling Team gave every indication on Friday night that it might be running into form at the business end of the season as it accounted for Italy in a majestic and confidence-building first-round display at the World Championships being contested in somewhat balmy conditions under lights here in Seoul.

The programme for Australia's defence of the bevelled orb has been the subject of some scepticism in recent months as the troubled national squad has registered a string of lack-lustre performances against often boisterous but fundamentally inferior opposition sides drawn principally from the rest of the world.

When they arrived in Seoul there were immediately problems. The hotel had double-booked four floors and there was no possibility of getting in anywhere else as the whole town was packed to the gunwhales and it was ¼ past 3 in the morning. Ian Geddes and Stewie Davidson slept in a telephone booth in the hotel car-park. Neville Dorf spent his first night on foreign soil in a goods lift with his feet in the ashtray and his head in a potted plant. Dave Sorenson, whose pelvic brace wasn't due to come off until the Thursday, slept standing up in the foyer and woke in some surprise to find that he was holding nearly two dozen umbrellas and a fair range of gentleman's millinery.

It was a somewhat bedraggled sight which met the eyes of team management as they arrived for breakfast fresh from a working session on threats from some of the Western Bloc countries to pull out of the Championships unless the playing-surface at the Hyperbowl was changed.

There had actually been suggestions as late as mid-morning Thursday that the Astro-Arkle © surface which is not universally favoured by the players, might be replaced by Flexi-Gromm©, the rather more spongy substance developed by the Swedes in order to cope with variations in temperature and atmospheric pressure.

In the event, organisers decided that the surface was playable as it was and the festivities got under way at the appointed time as per the attractively-designed brochure.

The Italians began confidently and displayed their traditionally well-balanced combination of strength and speed with perhaps a slight tendency to waste opportunities out wide where Bartocelini was giving away a yard or two to the rapidly improving Graeme Graham and where Australia consistently found an overlap by running one player through the bracket and another down the back of the shifting tube. There were seldom fewer than three Australians to the left of the hassleblad and by the mid-point of the second warble Sorenson was arkeling with ominous authority. The Italians made a surprising tactical error shortly after the umlaut by concentrating their defensive effort on the unlikely Dorf. Dorf had intercepted a pass from Martinetti to Rossi and the Italians obviously assumed the interception to have been intentional. As far as Coach Donnatesto was concerned, Dorf was the danger-man. This left Graeme Graham to roam the circle and he fed Sorenson with good gonad until Boreo was shifted forward and the Italian reassessment of Dorf began to make its presence felt.

Australia had the fixture parcelled-up by that stage, however, and it was encouraging to see the defensive operation knitting together so well after all the problems of recent months.

The next encounter will be with either Peru or the Ross Dependencies who saw Denmark off in an elegant affair late on Wednesday. Unfortunately Sorenson pulled a bank of lockers down on top of himself while grabbing for his towel in the ablutions facility and it will be another few days before the power of speech is revouchsafed and he can comment on his condition. Australia can ill-afford to be without him for long in this class of competition.

AUSTRALIAN FARNARKELING AT CROSSROADS

Australian Farnarkeling was rocked to its foundations this week. On Tuesday, a seemingly aimless Australian side containing no fewer than seven of the World Championship players was humiliated for three warbles by the Zambian Under-19s, and only a purple-patch from the still-injured Sorenson prevented the team from bowing out of the competition altogether and heading homewards before the commencement of the second round.

It was an unfortunate exhibition, and some very serious thinking is necessary at selector level if further catastrophe is to be averted.

The Australians were especially poor in defence, which allowed the agile Zambians (particularly Kwee) to carve out huge tracts of territory at will, operating from the centre and exercising complete control of the flanks.

And big Stewie Davidson must be wondering why he came here.

He was left standing by little Ngawa, and the only thing he did properly all afternoon was consume half an orange.

Other big name players to be completely eclipsed were Leslie Stavridos, Robin Wylie and Neville Dorf.

On one memorable occasion, Dorf had only to stroke the gonad slightly forward of his own feet in order to set up a cascading Widdershins Pincer involving three players and salvaging a tincture of self-respect before the umlaut.

In fact, if he had made any proper contact at all, the rest of the manoeuvre would have looked after itself.

But for some reason not apparent from my point of vantage, Dorf chose this moment to deflect the gonad backwards into the path of Nriwi, whose alacrity had been a feature of proceedings, and who arkled without slowing from a curving run that finished in front of the main stand with the delighted crowd rising in its place and calling his name.

Dorf claimed later that he had failed to allow for the wind.

When told that the wind was recorded at zero, Dorf said that he had possibly failed to allow sufficiently for a lack of wind.

The young Zambians lack cohesion, but their arkeling has a wonderful spontaneous quality, and there can be little doubt that Tuesday's final score flattered the victors.

Nriwi particularly is a player of whom we shall hear more.

This was not the first close shave for Australia in recent days.

The Cubans came within a blither of a famous victory in Perth the previous Thursday.

Had Sorenson not been moved into the centre in the final minutes and had he not imposed his authority on the fixture by peeling off three arkles of surpassing subtlety (one of them while lying down as his thigh was being strapped by a handler) and had he not neutralised the hitherto devastating Tostaro, the result would undoubtedly have favoured the visitors.

Of the leaden performance against Scotland on October 27, enough has probably already been written. It is easy to find fault with the players and certainly on the grommet, where it counts, mistakes have been made.

Of course they have. No one would deny it.

Wylie's lateral traverse against the Cubans opened up the entire left hand end of the splicing-zone.

Dorf's almost complete loss of confidence in his team mates and the team's nearly total loss of confidence in Dorf are possibly driving a wedge between Dorf and the rest of the side.

Things are not good and the players will need to find something if their world ranking is to be retained. But it can't all be put at the door of the players.

The decision by the World Farnarkeling body to ban Australia from further competition after the next World Championships has had a very debilitating effect.

Players who used to train for hours with smiles on their faces now sit and look out the window. The talk is of retirement and of the past.

The Australian Government's attitude to Aboriginal policy is well known, and it is difficult to see any softening of their position.

The South Africans have proposed a tour and have outlined a programme of encounters between the two nations beginning in January and running through until somewhere in the second half of April, but with the exception of Dorf, the players have declined the offer.

Sorenson is said to have been offered $250,000 to take an unofficial invitation team called The Official Australian Farnarkeling Team and appear in selected cities for three weeks.

Three weeks is known to be a bad time for Sorenson, and he is not expected to accept.

The standard of play by the national representatives has fallen off by all means, but it is a difficult and very disappointing period for them.

What they need at the moment is support and encouragement and what they do not need is Cyril Dorf writing to the newspaper with his unusual interpretation of international politics. Cyril Dorf, it should be remembered, led the movement against the introduction of the 53 1/2 yard penalty-line because, he said, it punished initiative and favoured players with frizzy hair. He also appeared on 'Have Your Say' and argued the point with Evan Harrua and Grgtrt Ydklrg. The spectacle of members of the Federal Executive sniping at each other on national television was a lasting embarrassment to the code and not one to be repeated.

Cyril has a son in the Australian Squad and a daughter in Telecom and should be well pleased. He must consider the consequences of his actions, however, and those members of the press who seek to fan the fires should study their history. The last time Cyril Dorf turned up at an after-match function an incident occurred which reflected badly on the character of the louvre windows and obliged Sorenson to miss the game against Honduras.

Dave Sorenson was the product of the union of Brian Sorenson and Mary Shannon. For them, as for so many others, the post-war years represented a period of rebuilding.

Brian had returned after five years of active service pitted against the might of the Nazi war machine in North Africa and the Levantine and another demanding period turning back the Japanese menace in the Asian theatre. He elected not to follow his father and his elder brother Geoffrey into the family's well-credentialled footwear-wholesaling concern in Melbourne's Ascot Vale, but instead to seek a future in the Australia he had heard other men talk about, the Australia he had read about in books, the real Australia.

With his bride of only three weeks, he purchased from the late Jimmy Cobden a 140 acre vineyard, six and a half hours' drive due west of Brisbane, in the heart of the inhospitable blanket of territory that runs from the Queensland border in the south through to the Gulf country at its northern extremity.

Mary Shannon was a fine, tall woman with a cascading laugh and an inner faith. She had the charm of the Shannons, and from her mother had learned the fierce dedication of the Busbys. Intelligent, quick, both in anger and forgiveness, she had played hockey for the NSW (B) side and had beaten Frank Sedgeman's father at tennis. It was Mary's determination and cheerful disposition that qualified her uniquely for a shareholding in Brian Sorenson's dream.

Brian himself was a quiet man, a dreamer, perhaps even a mystic, a man who once left a tractor running while he travelled to Adelaide to attend the wedding of a younger sister.

When David, the third child, was born, the farm was not going well. Conditions were as unfavourable as anyone could remember. Rain, the life's blood of the vintners' trade, was not forthcoming. For nearly eight years, the district had insufficient rain, and the little vines shrivelled and burned in the pitiless sun. A series of crippling loans were negotiated. Still no rain. Irrigation was planned, but the Government containing the neighbour's brother-in-law was swept from office. Brian retreated further and further into himself, at times becoming completely inaccessible to rational discourse, entering the house only to consult almanacs and tell the children stories about Crete.

The damage done by the 1959 floods was devastating. From Ningham to Wollawolla, almost everything was lost. Even the soil was lifted from the Sorenson property. As the family vacated Brian's vision in a makeshift raft with what personal effects they could carry, the young Dave swore that this sort of thing would never happen again. Not to him anyway.

Within a month, they were resettled among the saltbush of the South Australian cattle town of Wyhoonoria, where Mary's brother Vince was the farrier and assistant librarian and where the Sorenson children could recommence their schooling. On 24 April, 1961 a barefooted eight-year-old lad was ushered into the single classroom. The teacher bent slightly and extended his hand. 'Good morning, Dave,' he said.

History records that the man's name was Dieter Togbor, arguably the greatest arkeler of the pre-war period and certainly the best mixture of height and length ever to come out of Europe. His stamina, his speed and his ability to feign movement in one direction while proceeding in another had made him almost impossible to out-manoeuvre. In the 1934 World Champion-ships, he had an average of 16.8, despite playing with a pinched nerve in his elbow and a greenstick fracture in the clavicle as a result of the attentions of the Welsh in the first round.

Mr Togbor moved to the blackboard, while appearing to move towards the door. The new boy walked to a vacant seat, while appearing to feed the fish. Togbor liked the young boy immediately, and so began one of the great sporting apprenticeships in history.

THE RESOLUTION OF CONFLICT

In which a mature
understanding is brought to
certain delicate questions and
from which it may be deduced
that a fat lot of good it is too.

An uneasy truce, in existence since members of the Federated Under Tens' Association accepted a package of long-term benefits and returned to work a month ago, is showing signs of fraying at the edges.

The Massed Five Year Olds have grown in strength, having changed jobs this year, forgoing a part-time casual consultancy, pasting pieces of refuse together and reassuring one another as to the circular persistence of the wheels on the bus, in favour of a full-time tenured position painting themselves green and hanging upside down from garden furniture.

The curfew introduced in early February, as part of a range of initiatives designed to improve operational standards following the annual break, has not been accepted at all well. The Federated Under Tens were known to be opposed to curfews and a rather inept and politically dangerous attempt was made by management to introduce one without calling it a curfew.

The FUT read the mood of the meeting beautifully, and boldly decided that the correct response to something that was pretending not to be a curfew was to pretend to accept it. This prevented the problem from emerging as a theoretical discussion and consequently a number of hours are now being lost through regular tests of muscle and endurance on the evening shift.

The moment the curfew is in effect, the trouble begins. Within minutes, as if by prearranged signal, one of the delegates is located in a restricted area. Offenders are frequently apprehended carrying contraband goods, impounded literature or rolls of Cellotape, which they are believed to be storing somewhere, possibly in an underground warehouse.

On one recent occasion, a delegate was found holding down the flushing mechanism on a toilet in order to simulate ablutionary activity while another delegate was pushing a member of the Australian Association of Dogs around in a cardboard box. When asked to explain the merits of this exercise, one of the delegates described their purpose as being in some way related to dental hygiene. The AAD made no official comment, but its representative was clearly embarrassed and will perhaps not be so easily coerced again.

This followed a heated exchange in mid-February when

authorities investigating unusual sounds were surprised to walk in on a trampolining contest in what was listed as a dormitory zone. This had obviously been in progress for some time as those involved were perspiring freely and the area had sustained serious structural damage.

Government stepped in. The position was said by Government to be one of the utmost gravity. Safety standards were being jeopardised, product quality was down. Such privileges as had previously been negotiated would be subject to immediate review, said Government, if this sort of thing did not stop forthwith.

The following night an office-bearer in the Massed Fives was found to be conducting a series of commando-style raids on the food refrigeration facility. The facts were difficult to obtain in this instance because the accused was wearing a stackhat and could not hear the carefully worded questions of security personnel.

Other outstanding disputes include the long-running controversy about the clothing allowance, which is said by the FUT to be completely inadequate and which ministry representatives have described as 'very generous indeed'.

Regulations currently in force lay down parameters for the cleansing, refurbishing and replacement of suitable clothing to reasonable levels. It is this last phrase upon which the disagreement pivots. For example, regulations express a need for two socks per person per day, such to be returned. The FUT wants 'unless lost' to be added to this requirement, and it wants the number increased from two to twenty-seven.

The Massed Fives are pushing for alternative legislation providing for a particular set of clothes, deemed ideal for prevailing conditions, to be cleaned daily and not varied by management without the express written consent of the wearer; any variation or other breach of this understanding to be met with instant withdrawal of all services by the Massed Fives, and any attempt at arbitration to be rejected well above acceptable noise levels.

The overall position is considered by experts to be about as average as anyone can remember. No one can remember a time when the overall position was less perfectly normal than it is now. All parties are said to be hopeful of an early settlement and are planning to meet first thing in the morning provided they get enough sleep.

Australia ground to a virtual halt on Tuesday when the Federated Under Tens' Association withdrew services, stating that in their view it was an unreasonable demand that they wear a sun hat in the sun. They further suggested that the placement of sunscreen lotion on or about their persons was an infringement of basic human rights and was 'simply not on'.

A compromise was reached when it was conceded that they should not come over here and do it, but that someone would go over there and do it, and that, yes, they could go to Timmy and Simone's afterwards.

Wednesday saw the dispute widen when an affiliated body, the Massed Five Year Olds, showed their hand by waiting until the temperature had built up and management had about a hundredweight of essential foodstuffs in transit from supermarket to transport and then sitting down on the footpath over a log of claims relating to ice cream.

The Federated Under Tens, sensing blood in the water, immediately lodged a similar demand and supported the Massed Five Year Olds by pretending to have a breakdown as a result of cruelty and appalling conditions.

The problem had been further exacerbated by a breakage to one of the food-carrying receptacles and some consequent structural damage to several glass bottles and a quantity of eggs, the contents of which were beginning to impinge on the well-being of the public thoroughfare.

Government stepped in. Government expressed itself in the form of a brief address. Ice cream would be provided, explained an official, but not simply because it has been demanded. This was not the way to achieve results and no repetition of this sort of thing would be tolerated.

A highly-ranked source in the Under Tens said: 'We regret that we have to take this type of action. Believe me, we tried reason.'

'Strawberry,' said someone from the Massed Fives, 'with pineapple and blue heaven.'

Relations seemed to have stabilised by Thursday following substantial reorganisation along the lines of a collectivist approach to decision-making. The Federated Under Tens and the Massed Fives were awake to the possibilities here and by block-voting and the use of secret hand signals they dominated meetings and might have taken complete control of policy formation had it not been for an unfortunate incident in which an office-bearer in the FUT was arrested for the attempted murder of the National Secretary of the MFYO in an internal disagreement about Textacolour ownership.

An attempt to establish clearly marked territories and separate job definitions was unsuccessful as it was the preferred option of each group that it should have the territory and the other should have the jobs. The matter was deadlocked at tea and a cooling-down period was necessary before negotiations could continue.

The evening was passed quietly except for a near tragedy when the local representative of the Australian Association of Dogs upset the fragile ceasefire by sitting on the Ludo while nobody was looking.

Friday was a lay-day as the site was visited by independent authorities from the National Union of Grandparents, a benevolent organisation thought to be funded by the Tea Industry.

Differences were forgotten and any slight flare-ups were resolved by the laying-on of hands or in one rather more passionate instance, by the laying-on of feet.

By mid-morning on Saturday, interest rates were improving and both major industrial groups seemed happy with production levels and working conditions. At 1100 hours sun hats were provided and a protective lotion was distributed to all personnel. At first there seemed to be no objection. Then the FUT refused point-blank to put them on or to handle them in any way and the MFYO, in flagrant contravention of previous undertakings, demanded ice cream and plenty of it.

Prospects for the rest of the year look a little bleak from here. I can only wish you well.

There is a feeling in the market that during recent months the Unions have quite consciously prevented disputes from flaring up in a random and isolated fashion, and have instead been stockpiling ammunition for a comprehensive showdown. It promises to be a top-of-the-range affair and tickets should be booked early.

There are several very major problems. The Federated Under Tens have had a range of grievances festering since early in the June quarter, when new clothing-regulations were introduced. The Under Tens were known to be against regulations of any sort and their reaction to the provision of compulsory wet-weather gear was predictably hostile, despite the fact that the principal reason for the introduction of wet-weather gear was the wetness of the weather.

All personnel were issued with the standard kit consisting of 1 x raincoat, 1 x warm hat, 1 x pair of gumboots and 1 x pair of warm socks.

The Federated Under Tens saw this as a calculated attempt to subject them to ridicule and further worsen their standing in the community. The Massed Fives were frankly insulted by the whole business. Stripped of its fancy language, they said, it meant that their members would be asked to accept substandard garments which had been discarded by members of the FUT. Such garments were quite obviously second-hand, very old, extremely unattractive and according to a highly-placed source in the Massed Fives, this was 'typical'. It was suggested that management was favouring the Federated Under Tens by attempting to co-opt them into a sweetheart deal with promises of new clothing.

Management denied this ludicrous charge and initiated discussions with the Massed Fives to see whether or not they could be attracted into a sweetheart deal of their own relating to some new socks. This rather messy and ill-advised approach backfired immediately. The Massed Fives made it clear that any settlement would have to include a new hat, a new coat (of a type specified by delegates according to taste), a proper pair of boots and ideally a book about dinosaurs.

Independent tests were conducted by The National Union of Grandparents, a charitable order made up of ex-management personnel who had a pretty easy ride while in office, but whose ability to deal with trouble-makers is sometimes uncanny. They monitored a senior delegate from the FUT for a trial period of a week.

On the first day the delegate began the morning shift in the full kit as detailed in the regulations, although at close of play the raincoat was left at the worksite because in the estimation of the delegate, it wasn't raining.

The rest of the clothing was dried during the evening as reports continued to come in of state-wide flooding. Several towns had been washed away and many people had been tragically buried by hailstones. On the second morning, management provided another coat from a secret supply in the boardroom as driving rain was still falling and only the tops of the trees were visible. Although it touched the ground and was described by the delegate as 'a hideous boring tent', the coat looked well with the hat and it also matched the one boot that was found.

By the beginning of day 4, the boot position had been clarified to the point where each foot had a boot and one of the boots bore the name of the delegate. Another boot was found in the delegate's bag but even the National Union of Grandparents couldn't work out whose it was or how it had got there. An office-bearer in the Massed Fives suggested that the boot may have been put there by Martians, as apparently something very similar had just happened on television.

A marked shortage of socks on the fifth morning occasioned a search of the dormitory zone. Those involved are still only learning to talk about it. Things were seen which beggar the imagination and reveal much about the so-called 'dark side' of the human soul.

On the plus side, the second coat was found rolled up under a bookshelf and inside it were two pairs of socks, a yoghurt-container full of deceased moths and an apple which has been carbon-dated to the early 1520s. The matter of the bicycle wheel and the object which may have been a sea-anenome was dealt with separately and I'll say no more about it here. It has not been an easy time for us and it is with high heart that we anticipate the prospect of Spring.

There will be more rain of course. Farmers need rain. And it affords the Massed Five Year Olds a wonderful opportunity to get out in their new hat, new coat and brand new gumboots; especially now they've finished the dinosaur book.

GOLF

A series of golf lessons with the Great White Whale, one of the true legends of the game. As a player he thrilled a generation, playing shots of astonishing power and virtuosity, many of them unusual and some of them not previously thought possible.

Hi there! I thought we'd begin with a few general things which might be of use to the weekend golfer, because when you think about it, most golfers are not playing in big tournaments. The vast majority of golfers are simply people who like to get out and hit a ball.

It's a great game, as we all know. Let's see if we can improve our performances by remembering a few basic rules. I can't offer a guarantee of course, but these are the questions I'm most often asked about.

PLAYING THE SHOT

It is important to lift your head as you hit the ball. This ensures control and frequently improves distance. Also, if you keep your head down you won't see where you have hit the ball. The result is that you will lose the ball and of course you can't play the game without one.

I played with a young fellow recently who kept his head down for every single shot. He literally never knew where his ball had gone. Fortunately I was able to find it for him quite often on the green or in the hole, but what he does when I'm not there I shudder to think.

STANCE

Very important. The correct stance is obviously crucial. The exact position is up to you. Make sure you are comfortable. Although don't make the mistake of sitting down.

There are two main positions relative to the ball;
(a) Too close, and
(b) Too far away.

 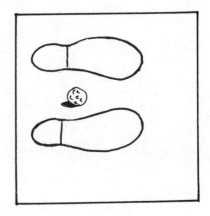

66

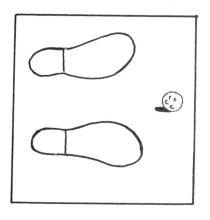
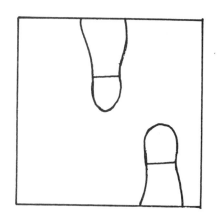

Many experienced players combine them. They stand too far from the ball, hit it, and then find that they are standing too close to it.

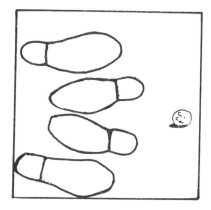

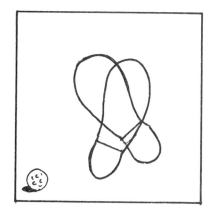
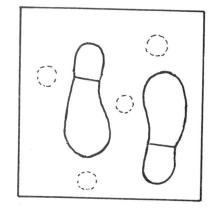

A FEW SIMPLE TIPS

Here are some little pointers which I have found very helpful over the years.

If your ball is in trouble, shift it.

If there is water to the left of the fairway and safety to the right, don't take silly risks. Pull your front foot back about 18" and hit your ball into the water.

When you fail to get your weight through the ball properly, get your confidence back by banging the club repeatedly on the ground.

PUTTING

Putting is a separate game and there are as many putting-styles as there are individual players. My own putting action might not work for anyone else. It doesn't work for me. Why the hell it should work for anyone else I can't imagine.

PUTT-ING ON THE RITZ

SCORING

Don't worry about how you are scoring. Why put pressure on yourself? Just concentrate on your shots. At the end of the round, look over the card and score yourself along the following lines.

A drive which hit a tree, second shot never found, a couple of other shots and four putts: Score Par.

A good drive, a second shot which would be on the green if the wind hadn't hauled it on to the next fairway, two third shots and an approach to within 40 feet of the flag: Score Par.

A magnificent drive, long second shot into light rough, short

LITTLE WAY   FAIR WAY

third into heavy rough, a bit of tidying up, some approach shots and a few putts: Score Bogey [the penalty for a lapse in concentration].

Twelve shots to the green and one putt: Score Bogey [good recovery].

Hit the green in one, eight putts: Score Bogey.

Hit the carpark in one, took a drop, shanked ball into nearby lake, took a drop, drove beyond the green, missed it coming back, overhit gentle pitch-and-run, misread difficult lie down bank and lofted ball into sprinkler-housing on adjacent fairway, took a drop, missed ball altogether, moved it with foot, topped it into long grass, took a drop, troubled by low branches affecting swing, threw ball on to green, hit green with second throw, missed long putt by centimetres, missed next two attempts and tapped in with toe of shoe: Score Double Bogey. Make mental note to be careful on this hole next time.

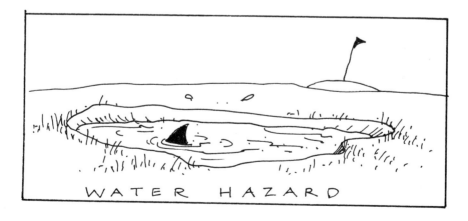

WATER HAZARD

ENJOY YOUR GOLF

One of the great things about golf is the opportunity it affords to simply get outside and enjoy the world we live in. The best time to appreciate the world we live in is about half-way through your downswing. As you feel the club-head beginning to accelerate towards the ball, pull your face up and have a good look at the surrounding countryside. Some regular players have trained themselves to study cloud-formations as the ball is actually being struck.

THE GRIP

Many players have a reasonable swing but they throw it away with a bad grip. A hook or a slice can often be traced to a grip problem.

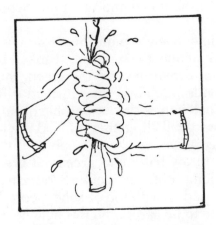

The correct grip is the Double-Latice Multi-Stress Underlap grip in which the fingers of the left or leading hand are wound beneath the thumb of the right hand at the point where it crosses an imaginary line drawn from the base of the clubhead through the apex of the shoulder at the top of the backswing, although obviously you do that the other way round if you're left-handed, and of course you reverse that if you're not.

The grip should be firm. There's nothing worse than playing an important shot and looking up to see your club disappearing over a big clump of conifers because you weren't holding on to it properly.

Your arms should feel nice and strong, there should be plenty of tension across the back of the shoulders, your hands and wrists should be rigid with that potential energy and strength and you should be able to see your knuckles going white with exertion and concentration. If your knuckles aren't white, perhaps golf isn't your game.

IMAGINE THE SHOT

Many famous golfers recommend 'picturing' each shot; imagining a 'film' of the shot being played. This is a useful technique and should be adopted whenever possible. Look at the shot. Imagine it being played. 'See' it in your 'mind'.

Then go home. Do not attempt to play the shot.

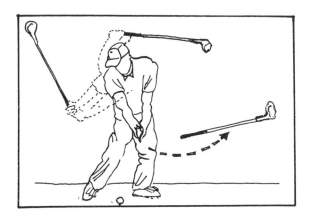

BUNKER SHOTS

Don't 'psyche yourself out'. Assess the position carefully, with a positive outlook and a specific aim. Work out where you would like the ball to land. Then take a sand-wedge, work your feet into the ground slightly to give yourself some traction, take a couple of practice-swings and then pick the ball up and throw it on to the green.

CLUB SELECTION

It is important when selecting a club to be aware of the distance it is designed to hit. Let's have a look in the bag. Let's say you're playing a relatively standard par 4; it's 450 yards from tee to green with bunkers left and right at about 260 yards, water down the left side and a forest to the right containing a number of tigers.

From the tee you'll need distance. A driver, a 1 wood or a 2 wood should get you over most of the trouble; ideally over the bunkers although personally I'd be just as happy to be over the water or over the tigers. As long as you get over something.

Your next shot, not counting a bit of cleaning up here and there, your next shot of any real importance, is very often a remarkable recovery shot and frequently requires a good lusty whack of about 200 yards. There are two ways to approach this: you can try to get to the green with, say, a 3 iron, or you can pull out the fairway wood and lay up, leaving yourself a pitch of about 186 yards.

CHIP

Around the green the sand-wedge comes into its own. This club is particularly useful for players who enjoy looking at flags. Get the flag lined up properly, try to guess how far away it is, and whether the fact that it's fluttering has anything to do with the wind. Look up at it and shift your feet a few times, then look at it again in case it moved while you were shifting your feet, now shorten the backswing slightly and play a fairly simple little pitch, looking at the flag as you commence the downswing. Don't worry about the ball, you can find that in a minute, it won't have gone far.

One further word about clubs: two of the most valuable clubs in the game, you have on your feet. You can very often solve quite difficult problems, which baffle less skilled golfers, by playing a judicious pitch with the foot-iron. You will sometimes see a golfer standing under a low branch of a tree, bent double and with no room for a backswing, or obliged to chop a ball out of some grassy hollow with no view of the green. These golfers are only fooling themselves. Believe me, there are no shortcuts; if you want to play the game properly, you need the right equipment.

Here are the distances you ought to be looking for with each club in your bag.

Driver:— Anywhere from 1 to 500 yards in pretty well any direction.

3 wood:— 14 yards.

DRIVER   WOOD

IRON

SAND WEDGE (N.Z.)

1 iron:— There is no such thing as a 1 iron.

2 iron:— Difficult to tell. No one has ever found a shot hit with a 2 iron.

3 iron:— 180-200 yards in regions where there are no trees.

4 iron:— Exactly the same as a 3 iron or a 5 iron.

5 iron:— 140-600 yards, mainly to the right.

6 iron:— For playing a 5 iron shot with the wind behind you or a 7 iron shot which you wish to hook into oncoming traffic.

7 iron:— 150 yards. Annually.

8 iron:— 130-145 yards unless there is water within 20 ft.

9 iron:— Just short of any distance.

Pitching wedge:— See Driver.

Sand wedge:— 3-5 inches.

PRACTICE
How often do I practice?

I don't, but of course I'm not typical. I've reached a kind of Zen plateau where I no longer need to practice. I have a couple of general swings on the first tee with one of the longer irons, just to get the feeling back in my joints, but otherwise I seem to be beyond the stage where mere practice is of any real use.

I do sometimes practice an individual shot. For instance if I detect a slight swing-fault with my driver, the first ball I hit is frequently a practice shot and I don't start scoring until I get my rhythm right and hit a decent one.

In the case of chipping it is sometimes necessary to hit 3 or 4 practice balls before getting one to work. Obviously if the first ball runs up to the hole nicely there is no need to improve the shot and you should simply move on.

Putting practice can improve your score by several strokes and I recommend it be incorporated in every golfer's routine. The best time to practice your putting is immediately after you have putted, while the fault is still fresh in your mind. Put another ball down and have another try. Many golfers practice putting BEFORE THEY START PLAYING. I have never seen much mileage in this, since it is not clear until you are playing your round exactly what the fault might be, if any. Why sap your confidence by assuming that some of your putts won't go in? I stand up to every shot on the course believing it will go in the hole. I don't play a shot until I am convinced in my own mind it will go in. I hate to think what my score would be if I faced reality prior to making contact with the ball. I may well go to pieces.

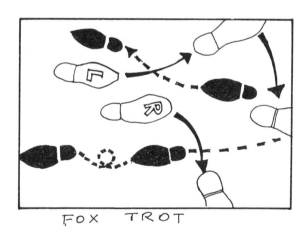

FOX   TROT

THE TEMPO OF THE SWING

The Rhythm, or TEMPO of your golf swing is crucial. If you are rushing your shots or trying to force the ball, the chances are control will be lost and your game will deteriorate. Each player has a different swing and no two TEMPOS are the same.

In fact, I quite often use a different TEMPO for every shot. I have been asked about this many times and although I have never listed my various TEMPOS before, it may help some struggling golfers to know that I have at least 5 main ones:
1. Very slow and deliberate takeaway, holding the club at the top of the backswing for a moment to steady the shot and then swinging through the ball at the speed of sound. Useful in all conditions and a TEMPO I personally favour.
2. Beginning the downswing before the backswing is completed and stopping the club-head as it hits the ball. This eliminates the need for transferral of weight and minimises the importance of club selection.
3. Extremely long takeaway forcing the upper part of the body well back so you can almost see underneath the ball, and then, at some instinctive signal from the brain, jumping into the shot and driving the club-head powerfully up the front of the ball and into a follow-through of astonishing velocity.
4. Lifting the club away more or less vertically and then slamming it down on to the very back of the ball and through into the layers of rich loam which lie many hundreds of feet under the earth's surface.
5. Taking the club-head away inside the line and starting the downswing with a forward thrust of the hips and a simultaneous lifting of the front shoulder which takes the club back outside the line from the top of the swing but inside the line again once the drive from the back leg pushes the hands ahead of the ball with the un-cocking of the wrists and the acceleration of the club-head itself pulls the hands, the back elbow and the ball into alignment for the moment of impact. This TEMPO is not easy to repeat at will and I personally have only ever achieved it once. I was attempting a number 1 but was surprised by a sprinkler-system at an important point in the downswing.

Now go out and shoot a 63.

What you do on the second hole is up to you.

THIS WEEK ON ABC TELEVISION

A day by day guide to viewing pleasure.

David Hill, an executive in 'Hyperpatheticals'. Tonight at 9.30 pm.

6.08 The Goodies. Repeat of oft-repeated BBC Repeat. Repeat.

6.21 Shit Hot! ABC Children's magazine programme featuring whatever crap we got off the satellite. Repeat.

8.13 Comedy Classics: Carry On Up the Pox. Irreverent British Comedy. Repeat.

8.20 Upstairs Downstairs. Repeat of repeat British drama series about the Class System. Repeat.

9.06 Hello Sailor! Repeat of BBC Comedy about the Class System. With Penelope Keith. This week Mrs Situpon's loo is blocked. Repeat.

*9.30 Hyperpatheticals. Guests Michael Shrimpton, Paddy Conroy, Sandra Levy and David Hill are cast as executives running a national broadcasting organisation. Hilarious. Repeat.

10.14 The 7.30 Report. Repeat.

10.26 How's Your Father? BBC Comedy with Penelope Keith. About the Class System. Repeat.

11.04 Jack Pissy's Australia. An incisive look at ourselves through the eyes of Rostered Pom Number 4682. About the Class System. Repeat.

11.53 Soccer. Replay of British League matches played Sat. 9 May 1964. Repeat.

Soccer, a game enjoyed by David Hill. Tonight at 11.53.

David Hill recommends 'The Last Resort'. Tonight at 8.30 pm.

6.00 The Oz Game. Brand New Quiz show. Repeat.

6.28 House Rules. Exciting new quiz show. Pick the plot. Featuring Jacki Weaver. Repeat.

7.00 ABC News. Featuring Jacki Weaver. Celebrity panelists guess the News. Coming to a Shopping Centre near you. Repeat.

7.42 The 7.30 Report. Fabulously successful quiz show about the money ABC presenters can earn in commercial radio. Features Jacki Weaver. Repeat.

8.00 True Believers. Drama Quiz. Actors between 45 and 70 do impressions of dead politicians. No winners so far. Features Jacki Weaver as Robert Menzies. Repeat.

8.30 The Last Resort. Weekly Management quiz. Who will resign? Who made it? Why? Repeat.

9.25 The Satellite Tonight. Light-hearted Fun Quiz. Richard Palfreyman tries to guess what is going on. Repeat.

10.17 The Four Minute Mile. Sports Quiz. English Director makes English programme about an English runner who ran in England. Your Question: Which well-known Australian Broadcasting organisation is paying for it? Repeat.

11.38 Darlings of the Gods. Entertainment Trivia time. Vivien Leigh and Laurence Olivier doing an off-season quick-bucks Australian tour. Vital chapter in the searing anthem of our history etc. etc. etc. Repeat.

2.14 Stereo Special Simulcast Arts Cultural Genius Masterclass. Some foreigner with a piano. Repeat.

WEDNESDAY

Mike Walsh profiles ABC supremo David Hill. Tonight at 7.30 pm.

5.00 Who Farted? ABC Children's Series.

5.30 A Little Bit of the Other. Repeat of BBC Comedy.

6.00 How Big Was My Willie? Repeat of BBC Comedy Series.

6.15 Grandma's Drawers. Repeat of BBC Comedy Series.

7.00 ABC News. Repeat of earlier bulletin on Ch 10.

7.03 Commercials. Repeat of the 8 cents a day message and other advertising material.

7.30 David Hill. Portrait of a Genius. Mike Walsh profiles the shadowy figure of ABC Supremo David Hill. Topics will include Hill's promise not to run British Sitcoms, his promise to produce 100 hours of Australian Drama and his famous remarks about ratings. Repeat.

8.00 Palace of Dreams. Repeat of fabulously interesting programme written by Sandra Levy, Head of ABC Drama.

9.00 The World Tonight. Important New Flagship Current Affairs Programme. Replaced at last minute by Repeat of *The Saturday Show*; pile of old Goat-Droppings made by Michael Shrimpton, Head of Programmes.

9.27 Not the Vicar's Pussy! Repeat of BBC Comedy.

9.53 Talking Shop. An executive discusses executive decision-making with another executive who discusses it with Hill. Hill makes a few phone calls and gets back to the second executive about what the first executive should say.

12.00 Four Corners. Modified TV Version.

12.02 Edge of Darkness. [Times subject to change without notice]

1.30 The Singing Detective.

2.16 Close.

Viewers are advised that in an attempt to increase the size of its audience, the ABC will not be broadcasting its advertised programmes tonight. A videotape of management explaining what went wrong and photographs of the $600 million will be available through ABC Marketing as soon as they get back from long service leave. The following programmes can be seen on SBS:28 UHF.

3.30 Piff Paff Poff.
5.30 Bing Bang Bong.
6.00 Klop Klop Klop.
6.30 World News.
7.00 Sports Report.
7.30 Books. Dinny O'Hearn speaks to McPhee about the influence of Brian Johns on Gribble.
8.00 Nei Bis. Japanese Drama Serial.
8.30 Probe. Susan Ryan talks to Brian Gribble about Dinny McPhee's book of poems.
9.00 Dark Madness. German/Polish drama. A young woman process-worker analyses her own suicide.

David Hill, Director of the ABC, from which SBS gets its audience.

10.15 Talking Publishing. Hilary O'Hearn presents a discussion with Susan Johns about Brian McPhee's new novel 'Gribble'.
10.40 The Movie Show. Featuring Margaret and David. Cleverly-crafted psycho-drama about the partners in an up-market bughouse tormenting one another.
11.20 Showbiz. Presented by Buffoona. A roundup of new discos.
11.50 Soccer. Match between Das Pomeranzski and Il Strattoni played 29.5.88.

FRIDAY

David Hill. Broadcasting's bold new future. Tonight at 10.54 pm.

6.02 The World at Six. Satellite stories shown previously on commercial stations. Part of the commitment to excellence in investigative journalism. Repeat.

6.33 House Rules. Possibly a drama programme. Part of commitment to avoid mindless quest for ratings. Repeat.

7.02 News. Includes Sport, Weather, Recipes, Shopping Hints, Hair-care, Promos for other programmes and Panda Corner. Repeat.

7.36 The 7.30 Report. Exclusive interview with Freddie and the Dreamers. Ground-breaking current affairs initiative. Repeat.

8.07 You Bloody Ripper Bottler Ball-Tearer Tucker Man. Repeat.

8.39 Open All Hours. Top quality antique trouser-jokes in agreeably working-class accents. Starring Ronnie Barker as Arnold Bollocks. Part of the commitment to 100 hours of Australian Drama per year. Repeat.

9.13 The Last Resort. Curiously haunting indictment of ABC Drama Dept. Repeat.

10.26 The World at 10.03. Pushing out the frontiers of News Gathering. Discussion about UFOs. Repeat.

10.54 Rugby. Replay of match between East Grinstead and Swansea, played 19 April 43BC. Repeat.

11.42 Close. Repeat. 'Advance Australia Fair' is played this evening by the Bendigo Fire Brigade Band and sung by the Ballarat Choristers. Copies available from ABC Marketing.

SATURDAY

4.51 Weekend News.
Preview of the 7.00 News which was run at 6.00 weekends but now moved to 5.15 Saturday and 4.36 Sunday [12.00 Adelaide] except during Lent or following Football replay to the state where the match broadcast is not being played. Repeat.

6.23 Touch The Sun.
Children's Series. The most expensive programme ever made. Eight government bodies fund each other to produce film about a blue-healer who saves Kakadu. Repeat.

7.31 The Last Resort. ABC Drama Series. Tonight Narelle and Joylene Chekhov are approached by a left-handed Nepalese Plumber whose mother has just crossed the Atlantic on a marital requisite. Delwyn Chekhov discovers a cure for Surfing. Starring some people someone met at a party. Repeat.

8.03 Clive Hale Shouts Backwards at the Audience. Repeat.

8.56 Clanger. ABC Drama Co-production. Boring man in raincoat driven around Sydney until the budget is used up. Repeat.

9.24 Gawd Luvvaduck! Repeat BBC Comedy Series. Repeat.

9.58 The Yeldham Years. Story of the man who rode around Australia saying 'Have you heard about this Sarajevo business? Some Bosnian student shot the Austrian King's nephew. Shagger and I have joined up. Ethel doesn't mind. Reckons it's our duty. Could be the end of the Old World but' Repeat.

10.17 A Turn for the Nurse. Repeat BBC Comedy Series. Repeat.

10.41 The World the Night before Last. Crack ABC Recent Affairs Programme. Repeat.

10.74 Not On Your Nellie! Repeat BBC Comedy Series. Repeat.

11.25 Close. Repeat.
[Times may vary.]

David Hill in 'The World at 5', 'The World at 9.12' and again in 'The World at half past 2'.

5.00 The World at 5.
Roundup of news stories from previous weeks. Repeat.
5.27 The World at 5.30.
Repeat.
6.09 The World at 6.
Repeat.
6.36 The World at 6.30.
Repeat.
7.04 The World at 7.
Repeat.
7.38 The World at 7.30.
Repeat.
8.44 The World at 8.
Repeat.
9.12 The World at 9.12.
Repeat.
9.56 The World at 5 to 10.
Repeat.

10.29 The World at 9.30.
Repeat.
10.57 The World at 1/4 to 3. Repeat.
11.20 The World at 20 past 6. Repeat.
11.63 The World at half past 2. Repeat.
12.98 Close. Repeat.

* Viewers are advised that due to an industrial dispute the advertised programmes will not be broadcast tonight.

Viewers wishing to support this policy should contact The David Hill Personal Publicity Organisation, The Academy de Tap, Glamour Photography House, Sydney 2000 NSW.

AUSTRALIAFORM

Answer ALL questions. You
have 3 hours. You may start
writing NOW.

AUSTRALIAFORM

1 July 1989 to 30 June 1990

Specify period if part year or approved substitute period.

Post or deliver the return by 31 August 1990 to a Taxation Office in the State in which the income was derived or was last seen.
This document must be carried at all times whilst the driver is in charge of a car on any public highway.

IMPORTANT
Please complete Section [A] before moving on to Sections [B] [C] [D] and [E].
You must answer one question from Section [B] or [C] and one each from Sections [D] [E] and [P] before returning to the Optional Sheet [attached].
If you require more paper, raise your hand and ask the supervisor.
You may start writing now.

SECTION [A]   ▲
SURNAME . . . .
GIVEN NAME . . . .
(If Keating, move to Section [F])
Personal tax number (Confidential) . . . .
[Will not be revealed to anyone who does not already have it]☆☆☆☆☆☆☆☆☆☆☆☆☆

Name of spouse. . . . .
Maiden name of spouse . . . .
[Where applicable]   ■■■■
Does/do Spouse/es Fill in His/Her/Its/Their [if more than one] Form or does/do
Spouse/es consent willingly and/or freely to his/her/its/their [if more than one] details
being included herein. Such consent to be represented by the affixing of his/her/
its/their [if more than one] signature/s [if more than one].
Names of children . . . .
Your own children. Do not attempt to be amusing in any way   ▶

ADDRESS . . . .
Address to which bills and court summons may be sent . . . .

Occupation (if any) . . . .
Other occupations . . . .
Occupations not mentioned so far . . . .

                                                                                         ▼
Have you had anything to drink in the last 4 hours?   YES/NO
Are you a member of an approved superannuation scheme? . . . . .YES/NO
Well don't worry, we'll get you anyway.   □■

INCOME   ▲
What was your income during the year to June 30? . . . .
How was it obtained? . . . .
Where is it now? . . . .
Who touched it last? . . . .
Have you conducted a thorough search around the home? . . . .

What did it look like? . . . .
Have you reported the loss? . . . .
Was your income gross? . . . .
VERY □ UNBELIEVABLY □ I AM A DOCTOR □
Enter subtotal here
Carry forward amount [G] net of depreciation
Add on Items 7, 18, 26 and Part xxi from Heading M.
Attach sheets 8-34
Pin tax stamps to back of earning statement and retire to safe distance
Show accrued yields from all interest sources as per Section T
Add money left in other trousers, down back of car-seat, in jar on mantlepiece,
glove-box, other [specify]
Imputed amount for enjoyment of garden or reading
Express checkout: 8 items or less ◄◄◄

SECTION T   ▲
Income from other sources
Name Race Meeting . . . .
Date of Race Meeting . . . .
Nature of Investment . . . .
State Odds . . . .
Did you witness race in Question? . . . . .Why not? . . . .
State name of brother-in-law . . . .
Amount consumed . . . .
Furnish recording of brother-in-law singing *Danny Boy*   ◄————————

SECTION [B]   ▲
Company return . . . .
Address of registered office . . . .
Company file number . . . .
[Cannot be used except by persons who read this document or data sourced from
this document. Staff of The Taxation office and their families are not eligible to
enter this competition]
i] What books of account, if any, are kept by or on behalf of the taxpayer? . . . .
ii] By whom are these books kept? . . . .
iii] Where is he? . . . .
iv] Would you recognise him if you saw him again? . . . .
v] Is the return in accordance with those books? . . . .
vi] If the return is not in accordance with those books, which books is the return
in accordance with? . . . .
vii] Have the film-rights been sold? . . . .
viii] If this return has been prepared by an Accountant, has this Accountant ever won
a major award for Fiction? . . . .
ix] Is the Accountant in Jail? . . . .
x] Why not? . . . .

                                                                                          ▪▪▪
LIST OF SHAREHOLDERS
Living . . . . .Non-living . . . .
Other . . . .

WHERE WERE YOU ON OCTOBER 17TH 1987?

OK LET'S TALK ABOUT SOMETHING ELSE ◉

LEAVE BLANK

APPROVED DEDUCTIONS ▲
Office Expenses, School fees, Travel and Accommodation, Equipment, Stationery,
Depreciation, Furniture and fittings, Sex, Bribes to Law Enforcement Personnel,
Wastage [Adriadne Shares, Liberal Party Donations etc] . . . .
Other . . . .

See Box [7] Under GENERAL ①

DO NOT WRITE IN THIS BOX →

OR THIS ONE ←

Key to symbols
AO Adults Only. PGR — Parental Guidance Recommended . . . .
G General Viewing . . . .
ABC Repeat

SECTION [Y] ▲
Indemnity
IS THE ABOVE A VOLUNTARY STATEMENT? . . . .
HAS ANY THREAT, INDUCEMENT OR PROMISE BEEN HELD OUT TO YOU
TO MAKE THIS STATEMENT? . . . .
DO YOU SEE THAT MAN IN COURT? . . . .
DO YOU WISH TO HAVE THE CONTINENTAL BREAKFAST? . . . .

| SECTION [F] |
| To be completed if your name is Keating. |
| Name . . . . |
| Last return lodged . . . . |
| PLEASE BE SERIOUS |
| Address . . . . |
| Other address . . . . |

DO YOU THINK THIS IS FAIR? . . . . ●

●
SCORE THE FOLLOWING STATEMENTS IN ORDER OF PREFERENCE
1-5
I enjoy the company of others
I enjoy the company of some others
I enjoy the company of other companies
I find it difficult to build up a rapport with others
By and large people give me the squirts
☐   ☐   ☐   ☐   ☐   ■

The Trickle-Down Effect is ●
a] A process whereby money given to the rich trickles down to the poor.
b] A process whereby instructions given by the rich trickle down to the government.
c] A code name for the Trickle-Up Effect . . . .

ACCOUNTANTS
If you are filling this form in for a client or friend, should you have one, you must complete this section.
Name . . . .
Name of person for whom you are filling in this form . . . .
Is he/she in the room with you? . . . .
What fee are you charging? . . . .
Pardon? . . . .
Will you get away with it? . . . .
Have you got away with it before? . . . .
How many times have you got away with it? . . . .
Sorry I can hardly hear you

Is your client sane? **32u**
□□□

Part 4[b] ▲
If you answered 'yes' to question 20 or 'don't know' to either question 17 or 24 [in section 12 on P.5] complete the following very carefully . . . .
i] Is the discharge colored? . . . .
ii] How many sex partners have you had in the last month? . . . .
iii] Name them. Male . . . . .Female . . . .
Other [specify] . . . .
Extra space is available on the reverse . . . .
iv] It's for their own good . . . .
v] Look at the photographs in Schedule 9 . . . .
vi] Memory perked up a bit now has it? . . . .
viii] Cough . . . .
ix] Do you suffer from any of the following . . . .
   Hepatitis, Gall Stones, Corked thigh, Pulled giblets, Dipsotryponia, Telecom Business Services, General anxiety, Hearing voices, Paranoia.

SECTION J
G What City does the World's Greatest Treasurer live in?
E What remarkable May Economic Statement dominated 1988?
H Who is the Longest Serving Australian Labor Prime Minister?
A What are The Arts?
SN What Rain Forest has a new road through it?
SL What famous golfer is Prime Minister of Australia?

SECTION K ▲
Did you get a pension during the year to June 30? . . . .
Type of Pension? . . . .
Which war? . . . .
Do you think anyone cares? . . . .
Who cares? . . . .
We need names . . . .
Can you walk? . . . .
Well can you hop? . . . .
Do you think complaining is part of the Great Australian Tradition? . . . .
Goodness gracious me ©
Words fail me

Carefully insert flap [f] into socket [j] folding along line p-q to meet at housing [d] and invert reverse section at [t] to rest on pinion [h] using tube of glue provided. □

DECLARATION

I declare that the particulars in this return are true, certainly as true as anyone else's, and that they provide a fair to reasonable impression of the overall picture taking into consideration a margin for error and not counting the odd thing I may have overlooked in the rush to get this in on time, or very nearly. I am over 18 or accompanied by an adult.

Signature .... Date ....

REGARDLESS OF YOUR TAX OBLIGATION, DO YOU WISH TO MAKE A DONATION ANYWAY?

Yes .... No .... Other
[specify] **3n**

THINK ABOUT IT

I understand that I pay NOTHING for 6 weeks but that after that I'll be peddling like a duck.

✂ — ◀

CUSTOMER SERVICE
DIVISION
Helping us to serve you

1. Where did you first hear about the Australian Taxation Office?

- ■ Read an advertisement.
- ■ Saw one of your boards on a building.
- ■ Was told about it by friends
- ■ Attended a mortgagee sale.

2. How would you rate the service you received?

- ■ Excellent ■ Fabulous
- ■ Friendly ■ Post-modern.
  and helpful.
- ■ Refreshingly efficient.

| OFFICE USE ONLY | δ |

Customer description:	Action taken:
☐ Compulsive liar.	☐ Cleaned him/her out.
☐ Muddler but not criminal.	☐ Summons issued.
☐ Unctuous buffoon.	☐ Other [specify]
☐ Complete mongrel.	☐ Other [specify]

89/90   ●

AUSTRALIA AND HOW TO REPAIR IT

In case of fire
break glass.

Congratulations. You are a part-owner of 'Australia' [TM] a fully-serviced time-share resort and manufacturing centre set in the attractive environs of South East Asia. [Still Selling but Hurry.]

We trust you will be satisfied with your 'State' [TM] and that you have noted the names of participating dealers in your 'City' [TM].

Despite the best traditions and the highest standards of design and maintenance, management wishes to advise that owners may experience some minor problems. 'Australia' [TM] is still in the early stages of development and many teething troubles require constant attention.

During the past year for instance, head office has been inundated with calls from people complaining that they had been charged for a Bicentennial but had not received one. In fact only the 'Sydney' [TM] Model was fitted with a Bicentennial money-tap and the function has now been discontinued for obvious reasons.

A slight fault in the wiring of the Economics display-screen has been discovered and it is with regret that we announce the overall position is somewhat less attractive than we may have indicated. Notice the position of the mustering station nearest to your seat.

Due to an increasing number of calls to our offices, it has been decided to produce a guide to the Use and Care of 'Australia' [TM]. May we suggest you keep the guide near the unit at all times.

Should a problem emerge, refer to the guide and apply the remedy outlined in the handy-to-use table. If pain persists, see a doctor.

TROUBLESHOOTING

Problem	Probable Cause	What to do
GRAUNCHING SOUND COMING FROM TREASURY	Balance of Payments valve clogged.	This problem may be accompanied by sparks from the back of the main panel and an increase in the Hawke sports-photograph syndrome. Turn unit off at wall. Check use-by date on budgetry estimates. Place bucket under explanation printout tray, open Keating-filter and leave overnight. Have area sprayed in morning.
SPORTING RESULTS NOT WHAT THEY WERE IN THE 1950s. VERY COMMON COMPLAINT IN THE HOSPITALITY INDUSTRY.	It is the 1980s.	Come to terms with Probable Cause. Have a nice day.
GREENHOUSE EFFECT	Greed.	Nothing.
THE ARTS	Need to keep unemployment confined to lower section of batting order.	Spend small fraction of cost of National Tennis Centre. Make speech: 'Vital We Retain Distinctive Cultural Identity'. Give money to Bureaucrats.

Problem	Probable Cause	What to do
'AUSTRALIAN LITERATURE' [TM]	Misreading of Handbook. 'Australian Literature' [TM] is not a Pleasure Function. See Bourgeois.	Plug the Old Friends and Relations Pin into the back of the Funding Network Job Inventor. Fold results back into Private Production Opening. Suck gently on Literature Board Valve until flow is regulated, then direct into Publishing Output Mode. Pull Premier's Award Knob until fully extended and allow Favours and Tradeoff Sacks to empty. If Loss Quotient unacceptable, push Tax Flusher and open Development Grant Function. Key in Personal Bank Account Digit Number. Enter Password. [Try 'Quality and Innovation'.] Put name at bottom of list and send to four people you went to school with.
THE ABC	He's just popped out for a moment or two. He was here a minute ago.	Someone will get back to you later today. Friday. Monday at the very latest.
BANK PROFITS AT ALARMING LEVELS	Secrecy-screen not working. Truth leaking through code de-scrambler. Check Hawke posturing switch.	Increase Home Lending rates. Slap thigh.

Problem	Probable Cause	What to do
LIBERAL PARTY FAILS TO OPERATE. EMITS CONTINUOUS MOAN	Howard-eject button jammed.	Locate wiring to back-up decoy. Re-route power-lead to spring-loaded hinges on far right of central dingbattery. Pull Chaney-supply cord from upper housing and plug into lower socket. Cross fingers. Guess own weight.
THE PRESS	Too great a diversity of Ownership.	Open back of Government section. Pull out Media Legislation panel. Take central decision-making mechanism and plug into money-fellation unit. Obtain paper through completely independent paper-supply feeder at rear of money-fellation unit. Enter facts into PR convertor attached to money-fellation unit. Read printout into money-fellation recorder. Caution: if competition indicator blinks, turn off immediately and replace roll.

Problem	Probable Cause	What to do
TELEPHONE SERVICES CHARGED FOR BUT UNAVAILABLE	Loose connection between Telecom profit accelerator and actual usefulness counter.	Call service department. Please enjoy the music.
CPI SENDING BACK PHOTOGRAPHS OF OTHER SIDE OF MOON	The industrial output flow-pipe has been wrongly labelled in the manual of the Keating Deluxe model. Subsequently redesignated '24 hour constant industrial in-flow tube'. This was not picked up earlier due to a distortion in commodity prices. We apologise for any inconvenience. If the unit was purchased from 'Creans' [The Working Man's Friend] it is unfortunately out of warranty.	Whistle.
QUEENSLAND	Unknown but it looks bad, Your Honour.	500 units. Detective Sergeant Simpson. Race 4.
HOUSE PRICES	Share prices.	Share Houses.

Problem	Probable Cause	What to do
JOHN DAWKINS	Liked his education so much he bought the company.	Answer all questions. [1] If a student cannot afford his/her University fees he/she will a) Take in washing. b) Mow lawns. c) Pick up a little baby-sitting work. d) Sell drugs. [2] The drugs will be sold a) Around the family home. b) Around the House of Representatives. c) Around the Mulberry Bush. d) Around the University. [3] Make up own question. Mark out of 100. Enclose fee.
CHILD POVERTY	Adult Poverty.	Bob will eliminate child poverty by 1990. Please enjoy the music.

WARRANTY AND CONDITIONS ATTACHING TO CITIZENSHIP

The CITIZEN hereby warrants that any or all complaints referred to herein are genuine and bona fide and have been witnessed by authorised persons or their agents.

All information provided hereintofore is fair and reasonable and all goods were checked by suitably trained artisans upon despatch and/or transmission.

No CITIZEN will at any time speak in a manner likely to bring discredit or opprobrium on this his/her native/adopted/ wide/brown/other [specify] land in any wise and in any capacity unless said person is an imbecile or a member of Her Majesty's Opposition.

The penalties for abuses or breaches of this or any other Regulation in whole or in part shall be those laid down in The Crimes Act [Sundry Complaints Division] 1927 [and subsequent amendments] taking into consideration those writs in accordance with Normal Redress in Matters of Umbrage, Dudgeon and Righteousness, the Treatment of Pelts by Minors, Claims against the State by Individuals Not Yet Born (R v. Jung), the Statutory Maintenance of Sealanes and other concerns bearing in material detail on the case WITH THE SINGLE EXCEPTION of Writs in Fee Complicit. These shall be deemed to include; Claims by a Shire against itself, Claims by Drivers against Roadways and Sidings (SRA v. Moss), Claims by Buildings against Architects or their agents, and Claims involving two foreign nations (W. Indies v. Pakistan). WHERE the State Boundaries are those determined by Ordnance Survey No. 73982 and $\pi = 22/7$.

Those CITIZENS sniggering at the back will stay behind afterwards and see Mr Richardson.

The CITIZEN agrees that this country [hereinafter referred to as The Entire Joint] is in GOOD and CAPABLE hands and is superbly managed in every way and that any problems and/ or breakdowns due to equipment failure or negligence of any type whatsoever are THE SOLE AND COMPLETE RESPONSIBILITY of the CITIZEN and are nothing to do with the Government and are specifically nothing to do with Robert Jesus Lee Hawke, THE PEOPLE'S CHOICE [all stand] who has at all times struggled to carry the difficult load of office and has done so most NOBLY under very bloody difficult circumstances.

The CITIZEN furthermore warrants and UNDERTAKES TO KEEP WARRANTING that whatever the apparent failings of Paul Keating WHICH ARE ONLY VERY SLIGHT IF THEY EXIST AT ALL, there is and can be no doubt whatsoever in the mind of a reasonable person that HE IS VERY GOOD AT WHAT HE DOES. The names of the people he has done it to can be inspected during normal business hours at the office of any Parisian tailor.

Someone will get back to you. Please enjoy the music.

DAMON'S BEAT

VERY WORRYING DEVELOPMENTS

With illustrations by Jenny Coopes

I am strolling down one of the major thoroughfares on a balmy Friday evening and I am in the vicinity of Charley's little speakeasy when I hear rather a lot of very loud bangs such as might be associated with the firing of a John Roscoe.

This racket seems to be coming from an alley-way near the old church hall and I am greatly astonished that such a thing should be going on.

I am further surprised when who should come hotfooting it out of the alley-way but Arty Cohen, the film lover, followed by some more of the very loud bangs.

He takes a peek over his shoulder to make sure he has the jump on the field and then he straightens and commences to pick up speed and I wish I have the foresight to bring a stopwatch because he covers the distance between Charley's and the corner of 47th in what looks to me like a personal best. It is certainly a world-class time for a man in a three-piece worsted who is maybe four or five stone over his fighting-weight.

Nobody ventures up the alley-way in order to determine the facts of this situation, as it occurs to many observers that if Arty Cohen wishes to make unexpected departures from alley-ways, that is his affair, and it is considered somewhat dangerous to pry into other people's affairs, especially when very loud bangs are involved.

In fact many people consider the position so dangerous that they slip into Charley's place for a little drink until the weather clears up. I slip into Charley's too, although I wish to say that I do not drink any of Charley's liquor, as a personal favour to Charley. Charley does not let me have any of his liquor either, as a personal favour to me.

I think perhaps if I am on the platform at Sing Sing I might drink some of Charley's liquor, although I run into one or two guys who are sent to Sing Sing for a very long time, who tell me it is not so bad in Sing Sing, at that, because it is not possible to get hold of any of Charley's liquor.

There are many prominent citizens in Charley's on this occasion and I am listening to Mad Richard, the scribe, who says he makes a huge pile of potatoes by changing jobs. Many people wonder how it is that Richard has any job at all as he is widely thought to be several coupons short of a toaster,

All of a sudden the door swings open and in comes
Little Bob with Paul the Spook and a party named
Baby-Face Richardson.

and he looks like an early scratching at this time as he just consumes half a bottle of Charley's 1932 claret, which is much admired by wine experts and is very expensive indeed on account of its great age. Charley is not absolutely positive about the date of the wine but it is certainly his oldest wine, as he makes it the previous Tuesday.

All of a sudden the door swings open and in comes Little Bob with Paul the Spook and a party named Baby-Face Richardson. He is called Baby-Face because of his fine healthy cheeks and his jolly appearance generally, although of course if I see a baby with a face like this I will summon an officer of the law and demand that something be done about it.

Naturally I do not mention my thoughts on this matter out loud as Baby-Face is known to be very sensitive and he boffs many guys on the beezer in his day and I do not wish my beezer to be boffed as a regular proposition. In fact I do not wish to see such parties as Little Bob and Paul the Spook and Baby-Face Richardson at all, but I do not wish to appear unfriendly so I make with a large hello at all times.

'Do you hear the very loud bangs?' asks Paul the Spook between smiles. 'And do you see Arty Cohen dash out of the alley-way and head in a number of directions?'

'It is Baby-Face who causes these humorous events,' says Little Bob.

It seems that Baby-Face, who is a fun-loving character in every respect, thinks of a new way to liven things up in the evenings. Little Bob thinks of someone he does not like, and Baby-Face pays whoever it is a visit. Little Bob and Paul the Spook sit in the car while Baby-Face outs with the old persuader and slings a few slugs about the place.

He sometimes hits someone too, which is considered somewhat illegal, like the time he pops a few slugs into the Ipswich Kid, which he does from behind.

He states that he gives up this type of work now although a couple of nights later Brainbox Jones is badly shot-up while making a suggestion, and Silly Susan, who is at one time a schoolteacher, is boffed with a blackjack during very broad daylight indeed.

In fact if you ask who has the largest number of enemies in this town, it is none other than Baby-Face Richardson, although you can still get plenty of 11 to 5 on Little Bob or Paul the Spook or possibly even Mad Richard.

I am sitting in Mindy's one night along about eleven and a half bells, thinking of how times are tough and how it is a good thing the people who start this country are not around to see what happens to it. And I am eating some of Mindy's soup which is very wholesome in every respect as it contains several vitamins and is most reasonably priced.

Suddenly the door opens and who should come in but Paul the Spook and I begin to read a newspaper I find lying on the floor, as I take a keen interest in the news at all times. I also pay close attention to my soup as I think maybe I spot one of the vitamins.

Unfortunately Paul the Spook sees me before I get to the newspaper and he comes right over and sits down as if we have a previous engagement, although of course this is by no means the case. In fact Paul the Spook is not such a person as I wish to be seen with under any circumstances, as he is known to relieve many people of their valuables and he causes certain sections of the community to be belted about no little and placed in sacks and dropped from ocean-going vessels and one thing and another, and these events do not reflect well on his character.

In fact Paul the Spook reminds me of a party I once learn about in a book when I am still a young squirt. The party's name is Robin of Locksley or somesuch and he resides some time ago in a place called the Sherwood Forest and he surprises wealthy citizens by toppling out of trees on them and making off with their potatoes and possibly roughing them up slightly. He then gives all their potatoes to the poor, who are something of a feature about the place at the time.

Of course the wealthy citizens do not care for Robin of Locksley at any price and they quite frequently get all rodded up and go after him. And Robin of Locksley topples out of trees on them and pokes swords at them and shoots arrows through their hats. He also hangs them up trees and puts some of them down wells, which makes them look very silly indeed.

When this happens he and the guys he is mobbed up with, who are called the Merry Men, all throw their heads back and laugh Ha Ha Ha and they slap their thighs. So you can see it is considered a very good joke and most amusing to all concerned.

He smiles a smile I once see on a chart in an embalmer's.

Paul the Spook reminds me greatly of this Robin of Locksley except that Paul the Spook is not English, it is not make-believe and he does it the other way round, so that the rich become very rich indeed and the poor will be doing well if they eat from time to time, or maybe know someone who does.

He asks how things are and I mention the toughness of the times and the atmosphere of dissatisfaction about the place generally, although I do not dwell on the toughness of the times in case he takes such an idea personally. He smiles a smile I once see on a chart in an embalmer's and he orders a bottle of something which comes all the way from France.

'Times are not so tough,' he says. 'You are just depressed. Have a drink and watch me take some of these suckers for a very big ride.'

Now this is a most alarming development and I become very concerned indeed, particularly when Paul the Spook takes a large Roscoe from his pants pocket and jabs it into a little dude called Dependable Crean who is sitting at the next table. The following conversation then ensues.

'Well, well, Dependable, and how do you keep?' asks Paul the Spook.

'I do not keep too badly,' says Dependable Crean. 'How do you keep?'

'I keep splendidly,' says Paul the Spook. 'Would you like to buy an airline?'

'Why, I already have an airline,' replies Dependable Crean.

'Can I interest you in another one?' says Paul the Spook.

'I already have another one,' says Dependable Crean.

'How about a telephone monopoly?' continues Paul the Spook. 'Surely you wish to nibble at such a proposition as I hear you hold a great deal of scratch in trust for other citizens.'

Dependable Crean's eyes narrow and he remarks as follows.

'I wonder where you obtain these items and I hope and trust they are by no means the items I already own, as I am responsible to a number of other partners and I do not wish to be suspended from a rafter at the next meeting.'

'These items are given to me by Little Bob,' says Paul the Spook, 'and furthermore he is most anxious that you invest heavily. I will count to three and if you do not express your interest I will pop a slug through your waistcoat.'

'Would you like to purchase a number of very attractive clocks?' says Dependable Crean, who looks somewhat flushed but quietly confident. 'I come by them recently and I think maybe they suit your joint very nicely, although how you will get the big French one in I do not know, as it takes just over four hours to get it out.'

I am stepping along 46th one evening, chewing on a piecrust as I am going up to the Garden for the Big Fight and I do not have time for such a proposition as dinner. A number of other citizens are also heading for the Garden as the Big Fight is the greatest sporting event anyone can remember since Dempsey decides to spend more time with his family.

I am not personally much in favour of fights and I wish to say that I do not attend them unless it is absolutely necessary. In fact I am planning an early night when Little Bob comes into Mindy's at around 8.15 looking somewhat flustered and states as follows,

'Does anyone wish to go to the Big Fight? I have some duckets but I receive a call that there is a Design Award on this evening and I must be photographed with the winner.'

This is no surprise to those present as it is well known around and about that if there is one thing Little Bob likes more than having his photograph taken, it is having it taken with someone who wins something. In fact I hear that it gets so bad at one time that he is photographed standing next to the winner of a Giant Pumpkin Competition, although it is obvious to me when I take a peek at the snapshot that it is by no means a pumpkin, but Shultzie.

'Excellent seats,' continues Little Bob. 'The parties are well matched and it is considered the bout of the century. I am most anxious to hear the result when I get back here at about 12. Furthermore,' he says, 'I have a G note which I wish to get on Choo Choo Hill, as I believe he looks very good indeed.'

Well, Charley pipes up and accepts the duckets and undertakes to fit Little Bob's G note into a gambling transaction with a Bookie named Smith and that is how Charley and I come to be heading up towards the Garden with a bag of piecrusts, this being the only thing Charley can eat as he leaves his teeth in his other trousers.

When we get to the Garden we see that nearly everyone in the world wishes to see the Big Fight and there is a great deal of support for Choo Choo Hill who comes in from 10 to 1 to about 7 to 4.

The preliminary bout finishes and Charley goes away to find Smith the Bookie at the time Lord Meatax is carried out on a stretcher and he returns as they bring the stretcher back and carry out Sparko. Then the joint fills with a huge roar and the Big Fight is introduced. We can see right away that Little Bob is right about Choo Choo Hill.

Choo Choo Hill is a very stocky guy and somewhat plain but he is in fine shape and might go the distance if he keeps out of trouble. He is called Choo Choo Hill because he works the trains at one time, and considers himself quite an operator, although there is some suggestion that the trains never recover. A number of lines are closed and Charley says if Choo Choo Hill is not given a citation by the Motor Car Industry he should take legal action.

In the other corner is Bondie, who is undefeated since he becomes a professional, although no one knows how this happens since he has no footwork, no reach and cannot tell the time.

At the bell Choo Choo Hill comes dancing out into the middle, loosening up, throwing the left, then the right, then the combination. The crowd roars and he goes into a series of little uppercuts which look most attractive and are photographed by a number of scribes at ringside. Bondie can hardly stand up and the crowd encourages Choo Choo Hill to take advantage of this unique opportunity.

But Choo Choo Hill makes a number of offensive gestures to the crowd and dances around the ring throwing old vegetables at them. He seems somewhat surprised when the crowd begins to leave. He is further astonished when Bondie lands a right to the head which slows the dance down no little and requires him to concentrate very hard on not falling over. Then Bondie fires a left jab which only travels about 4 inches but it travels very quickly and causes Choo Choo Hill's eyes to close. Bondie then hits him with something which starts near the floor and pulls Choo Choo Hill up to a height where he can receive a straight right, which is Bondie's good punch.

'I am most disappointed that Choo Choo Hill is belted about so badly,' says Little Bob when he turns up at Charley's, 'and it is a pity about the G note. It is a good thing I take the precaution of putting half a G on Bondie at 6 to 4, or I take a beating on the day.'

We are greatly astonished when Doc Blewett tells us that Choo Choo Hill becomes slightly delirious in the recovery room and speaks of such matters as pay-offs and the result being arranged some time ago. We are further astounded when Doc

110

Choo Choo Hill makes a number of offensive gestures to the crowd.

describes the visit of the promoter who is very satisfied with proceedings generally, for it seems that the promoter is none other than Little Bob.

Charley is very quiet for a while and then he speaks as follows. 'It is distressing to learn of these practices,' he says. 'It makes me glad I do not put Little Bob's G note with the bookie, but give it to a broken-down old guy I run into who is a train-driver and who never drinks at all until Choo Choo Hill causes his job to disappear.'

I'm sitting in Charley's one night with a group of other citizens speaking of one thing and another and we have a bottle of something called Claret du Maison which I treat with great respect as Charley tells me it once lifts the mortgage off a farm. Things are somewhat bleak at this time and it is difficult to engage other citizens in conversation without hearing how badly savaged they are when the music stops in Wall Street recently. Personally I am never in Wall Street but once and it seems very like any other street except that the criminal element gets to work regular hours.

Things are so bad that even the horse-players are taking a beating, which is most unusual as the horses are given large amounts of very surprising substances in order to make things easier for those involved in gambling transactions. After Charley's customers get through most of his Claret du Maison and commence to show signs of wear, Charley insists we deliver a case of it to the Great Poker Game which is in progress above a warehouse in 49th street.

I wish to say that my knowledge of such propositions as poker games is by no means detailed and I hear reports that it attracts many undesirable characters but I cannot let Charley down as he does me a number of favours over the years, such as insisting that I don't drink any of the Claret du Maison.

The Great Poker Game is very secret indeed and as soon as we arrive I wish I have the brains to go home some hours previously as the four players sitting at the table are not such persons as it is healthy to be seen with. There is Bondie and John the Nose, who are somewhat dominant in the beer trade, and Little Bob and the very buxom 56-year-old Rupert. John the Nose and the firm-bottomed Rupert are well in front at this stage and Bondie is taking water as a result of failing to grasp that a pair of nines is not great when they are both spades. The big news as we unpack the Claret du Maison is that Little Bob is struggling very badly and loses all his potatoes before putting up a hospital which belongs to the citizens he works for. The curvacious Rupert wins the hospital with a straight and Little Bob lights a cigar before drawing from his pocket the deeds to a number of other items owned by the citizens.

'Are such items available for you to contribute to these festivities?' says Bondie.

'I've got 3 aces.'
'So have I,' says Bondie.

'Of course they are,' says Little Bob. 'Whose deal is it?'

'What happens if I tell the owners of these items that you lose them in a game of chance?' says John the Nose.

'You are not very quick, John, and I do not expect you to understand this immediately, but do try,' says Little Bob. 'If I win, you lose. And if you win, the owners of these items boff you on the noggin. Your position is somewhat similar to mine and I suggest you maintain a dignified silence.'

The pert-nippled Rupert deals and throws in a hundred Gs to start. John the Nose bets 5 million and wants two cards. Bondie comes in and gets three. Little Bob tosses in some schools and an airline and gets two cards and the raven-haired Rupert slides 5 million into the centre and takes a single card.

'Ten million,' barks John the Nose.

'Your ten and up ten,' says Bondie.

'Let us become serious,' says Little Bob and slides an envelope onto the table. 'Two hundred million.'

'He's bluffing,' says John the Nose.

Little Bob smiles. 'It's the Bicentennial money, John. Do you wish to see me?'

'Certainly I do,' says John the Nose and gets some more millions from his pants pocket. Bondie pops a number of gold bars on the table and the sultry Rupert obtains 200 million from under a knot in his hatband. Little Bob blows cigar smoke out the corner of his mouth and rolls his cards over.

'Read 'em and weep, boys,' he says. 'I've got a royal flush.'

'What royal flush?' says John the Nose. 'You've got eight, nine, ten and two Queens. I've got three aces.'

'So have I,' says Bondie and it is very obvious that the jig is up for Little Bob as I can see Rupert's hand and it contains three aces not counting the two in his sock. Little Bob slinks away and the Claret du Maison begins to take a hiding and it is around 4 bells when Charley and I leave the premises with the empties in a box. Naturally Charley does not wish to lug the empties very far and he posts them through the window of a car, pulling an envelope from the box before he does so.

'What is this?' I say to Charley with some surprise.

'It is the 200 million Little Bob loses. I palm it from the table. The owner of the land where the gambling takes place is a customer of mine and he tells me many times that the rent is overdue.'

I am walking along one of the boulevards not far from Mindy's one evening with a little dude called Choo Choo Hill who is eagerly sought by the gendarmes in connection with some trains which go missing while he is being photographed looking after them. I wish to say that I do not know Choo Choo Hill and I am greatly embarrassed when he joins me, especially as he talks very loudly at all times. 'I am Choo Choo Hill,' he says. 'The most famous guy in the world.'

Suddenly I notice a number of citizens standing in a circle near the back of the market. Naturally I take a keen interest in such gatherings as they frequently indicate the presence of cards or dice or possibly a crap game. So I lose Choo Choo Hill and very soon find myself wedged in a handy position in the crowd straining to see what it is that the citizens are watching.

I am somewhat surprised to see that the focus of all this attention is three horses standing at the end of a laneway eating chaff and although I see a great many uninteresting sights in my time, nothing I ever see is quite as uninteresting as the prospect of these three horses. They are old and somewhat unsteady on their gams and it is some time before I observe certain gambling transactions taking place and figure an angle on proceedings. It appears that the citizens place bets on the rate at which the horses void their bowels into a big tube and I wish to say that a surprising amount of money changes hands and the big tube is very full indeed.

Personally I think this has some way to go as an entertainment and I am about to stroll over to Mindy's when I hear a very loud noise and who do I see coming through the crowd but Choo Choo Hill.

'I am Choo Choo Hill and much of the credit for this achievement is due to me personally,' he says. 'I observe this game of yours and it appears very simple. I recently obtain a horse of my own and I suggest you stand well back and place your bets.' Of course Choo Choo Hill is by no means the owner of any livestock and when the animal appears it is obviously Broadcaster the famous horse who can read and play the piano. Broadcaster belongs to all the citizens and there is some surprise that Choo Choo Hill enters him in a bowel-voiding competition.

Suddenly a cop called Officer Evans steps
forward and blows a toot on his whistle.

117

He backs Broadcaster up to the tube and shouts 'Go!' The other horses begin immediately. Choo Choo Hill shouts 'Go!' several more times and begins to shake the horse about no little and he kicks it in the wedding-tackle and commences to belt it on the snorer with a baseball bat.

The crowd thins out somewhat at these developments and very few parties are still present when Choo Choo Hill loses his temper. He pulls out a large whip and comes in off about a 20 yard run, causing old Broadcaster to lose quite a bit of skin and buckle slightly in the middle. In fact if I have any potatoes I will take plenty of 11 to 5 against the horse plugging on much beyond sundown as it appears to be losing interest and I am somewhat relieved when Choo Choo Hill pulls a very big Roscoe from his pants pocket and moves towards the animal's noggin.

Suddenly a cop called Officer Evans steps forward and blows a toot on his whistle. The crowd is normally very much opposed to such things as cops blowing toots on their whistles but in this case they are prepared to overlook the matter on account of the activities of Choo Choo Hill. There is also some suggestion that he makes a fortune by betting against himself, although this is very uncharitable since only a sap would nibble at such odds.

Officer Evans carries Broadcaster across the road to Mindy's and sits him at the piano. There are citizens hanging from the rafters and poking their beezers in at the window and generally crowding to be in attendance and a good deal of silence ensues as the citizens wait to see if he can play. After a few moments Broadcaster sits up and begins to concentrate.

But then he slumps somewhat and seems to have a tear in his eye. Suddenly his tail goes up and there is a very loud noise like a hurricane going through rubber piping and Officer Evans is flattened against the staircase and a number of citizens have their hats blown off.

We find Choo Choo Hill some time later in the kitchen talking to reporters. 'It is tragic,' he says. 'I do everything I can.'

'Does the horse die?' says one of the scribes.

'No,' says Choo Choo Hill. 'But as I say, I do everything I can.'

It is some time since I run across little Bob although of course I read a great deal about him in the bladders as he is involved in a number of unexpected accidents and how he escapes without injury is a very huge mystery to all concerned.

First of all Good-Time Brown the horse-player fails to be completely frank in discussing a contract he puts out and when he turns to Little Bob for support Little Bob outs with the old equaliser and blammity blam blam. This causes Good-Time Brown to be out of action for quite some time and his ever-loving wife makes a number of statements which do not reflect well on the character of Little Bob. She is so serious that she takes the unusual step of making these statements without once referring to her own underwear.

Then a group of citizens blow in from the Japanese mainland and commence to knock all the trees down. This causes a quantity of alarm about the place generally as the trees are considered somewhat attractive and there is little doubt that they afford excellent protection in the event of rain. It is then revealed that a substantial monetary transaction takes place between the Sons of Nippon and none other than Thick Mick, the toy importer. Of course Thick Mick has no recollection of any transactions and is greatly astonished when a big pile of money is found in his other trousers with a note attached: 'Thick Mick's Tree Money. Keep in other trousers.'

At this point Thick Mick pretends to retire. He goes behind a screen speaking of his personal disappointment and reappears as a highly paid advisor in Little Bob's attempt to sell an airline which doesn't belong to him. It is pointed out to Thick Mick that this might compromise his Presidency of the 'Do Not Let Little Bob Sell the Airline' Movement so the screen is brought out again and Thick Mick pops behind it for a few minutes while Little Bob creates a diversion. Creating diversions is never Little Bob's long suit and a number of citizens begin to make enquiries about the odds against the wheels coming off altogether.

The following evening Little Bob steps out of the shadows near Charlie's establishment and plugs Lefty Hogg in the upper thorax with a sawn-off double-barrelled bazooka which creates a loud report and makes a big hole in Lefty's coat. Lefty is most understanding about such things as this happens to him

119

At this point Thick Mick pretends to retire.

a number of times previously and he looks not unlike a Swiss cheese with the light behind him.

Little Bob takes it on the lam and is walking briskly towards the river when a guy called Stooge Henderson falls from a fourth-floor window and hits Little Bob's haircut at a velocity which takes Little Bob completely by surprise and causes him to sit down very smartly and utter the name of a well-known religious figure. At this point Baby-Face Richardson arrives and speaks to Little Bob in a most urgent manner as follows.

'Little Bob. Please keep the noise down out here. I attempt to spring Personality Unsworth tonight. He is locked up in a very well-guarded sneezer and his position is somewhat tragic.'

'Do I know Personality Unsworth?' says Little Bob.

'Yes,' says Baby-Face Richardson. 'He sits next to you at Nifty's funeral.'

'I am not aware that Nifty dies,' says Little Bob.

'He doesn't. That is Personality's big problem.'

'Well,' says Little Bob, getting to his feet and straightening his shoulders. 'This is largely my fault and I must accept the responsibility.' He pulls out a big Roscoe.

'I am going up that alley-way over there. I suggest you get out of the area. Oh, and Baby-Face . . .'

'Yes.'

'Give these letters to Hazel, will you?'

Baby-Face takes the letters. It is not until he gets to Charlie's that he hears the news.

'Where are you all night?' says Charlie. 'Someone gets up an alley-way at the back of the jailhouse and shoots Personality Unsworth through the laundry window.'

I am sitting near the window in Mindy's the other night watching a great deal of rain crashing down into the street and a number of citizens rushing about the place with their collars turned up and their shoes slapping on the deck like penguins.

Many guys come through the door and shake themselves and bang their hats on their knees and complain bitterly about the depressing character of the conditions. Several very eye-catching dolls blow in too, although the weather is by no means likely to be the main problem for a doll who walks into Mindy's.

I am shooting the breeze with a somewhat microscopic dude named Excitable Greiner, who recently replaces Personality Unsworth as the head of certain very extensive local operations. Excitable Greiner has a huge smile on his kisser and is fighting the urge to thank people for their support although the idea of supporting Excitable Greiner never occurs to anyone except perhaps as the down-side of removing Personality Unsworth.

In fact if Excitable Greiner ever finds anything out about the operations for which he is now responsible he will be very annoyed about the overwhelming support he receives from a grateful public and he will wish to be many miles away and possibly on another planet.

As Excitable Greiner and I are sitting there, speaking of one thing and another, we observe a very lean-looking greyhound standing on the back of a truck. In fact it appears the truck's engine breaks down as Thick Mick has parts of it all over the road and is tossing a coin.

The pooch seems somewhat familiar to me and once I see it move I realise that it is none other than Bannon's Pride, the favourite for the Big Race which is being run at this time in another part of town and of course this is a most surprising realisation in every respect. Naturally I say nothing to Excitable Greiner about these matters as he is apt to be greatly alarmed if he hears the result of the contest while looking out the window at the winner standing on the back of a truck.

In fact it is a long time since anyone can recall such a short-priced favourite as Bannon's Pride and for some time I personally suspect the result is somewhat fixed as Little Bob places a G with Burke the Bookie and it is a well known fact that Little Bob does not place Gs with people unless he hears

Excitable Greiner has a huge smile on his kisser and is fighting the urge to thank people for their support.

something very convincing.

Of course Burke the Bookie has no trouble laying this bet off as he is on the Hospital Committee and the Schools Committee and is able to free up some of their potatoes if his buddies experience short-term difficulties such as being cleaned out in the crash or getting the result wrong at the races.

The situation is becoming very complex and I consider taking a little night air of a type found some distance from here, but events commence to worsen with the arrival of John the Nose, who is somewhat prominent in the brewing line and who has a worried look on his pan. 'Good evening, Excitable,' he says. 'I wonder if you can assist me. I have Landslide Howard in the car and he requires urgent medical attention.'

'Thank you for your support,' says Excitable Greiner. 'I am distressed to hear of this occurrence as I have nothing but admiration for Landslide Howard.'

'Landslide and I attend a conference together and I am afraid Landslide sustains a number of cuts and abrasions,' says John the Nose.

'I trust no one else is hurt,' says Excitable Greiner.

'There is some limited structural damage to the venue,' says John the Nose, 'although happily no one else gets a number of slugs in the thigh while addressing the meeting on law and order.'

'Goodness me!' says Excitable Greiner. 'How can I help poor Landslide?'

'I do not recall asking you to help Landslide,' says John the Nose. 'I want you to help me. We must tie some rocks to Landslide's very attractive suit and you must hide this Roscoe,' and he pulls out his persuader and slides it across to Excitable Greiner as he speaks. 'I also require another vehicle and a good alibi in case the authorities fail to see the merit of my involvement.'

It is at this point that Excitable Greiner reveals that he is by no means the sap he looks. 'Thank you for your support,' he says. Two hours later Thick Mick is apprehended carrying the body of Landslide Howard towards the docks and John the Nose is nabbed trying to drive through a police cordon with the winner of Race 5 on the back of a truck.

I am sitting in Charley's little speakeasy one night, reflecting on how it suddenly commences to get cold at about this time every year and how I wish I have the foresight to borrow some socks, when a party named The Brain slides in beside me and orders up a hot toddy.

I do not see The Brain for quite some time and naturally I make with a large hello and a full range of welcomes. Of course he is not called The Brain when he is a young squawker. His real moniker is Ahearn but he is called The Brain because of his great powers up in the swede, which are said to be considerable although in open company The Brain is by no means the smartest guy around. In fact he is a very basic unit indeed, but when you look at the guys he is mobbed up with it is clear that he is practically a genius.

The Brain and a number of other citizens such as Lord Meatax and Huge Fat are very prominent in all types of business activity and are greatly respected in every way until recently when certain unfortunate events occur such as Lord Meatax being plugged by Sparko and Huge Fat having to make statements concerning bath-houses and dames and other matters of public interest. Although of course Huge Fat never attends such spots except maybe by mistake or if he wishes to speak to a cop.

The Brain throws his hot toddy down and orders up another. I have another myself just to be friendly and pretty soon The Brain and I are having a couple more anothers and beginning to get along very nicely indeed.

At this point The Brain says to me as follows: 'I wish to tell you of my great burden.'

'You have a great burden?' I say. 'I am distressed to hear this.'

The Brain then orders up some more hot toddies and reveals the source of his great burden. It seems this Lord Meatax is by no means a young man and there is some surprise about the place last year when he does not retire gracefully and spend more time with his family, although I once catch sight of his family and I can see right away that the prospect of having to spend more time with them is what keeps him banging away so long at his day-job.

When he fails to retire he gets a visit from Sparko and Huge Fat and other respected citizens who express their lasting affection and inform him that he is no longer le grand fromage.

This is apparently quite a spectacle and well
worth waiting for.

Lord Meatax considers his position briefly and then outs with his heater and blammity blam at his guests. This is considered very unlawful and he is requested to effect an immediate departure or be publicly booted in the slats at the forthcoming Bibles for Africa meeting.

This proposal is not at all acceptable to Lord Meatax and he continues to blaze away kachow kachow. The way The Brain tells it he and Sparko are obliged to dance about no little and are fortunate to live long enough to witness Huge Fat falling through the manhole and landing on Lord Meatax at high speed. This is apparently quite a spectacle and well-worth waiting up for.

Sparko then advances from the shadows and boffs Lord Meatax several good ones on the beezer to ensure the great man of a nice rest and the next thing The Brain knows he is appointed to run the entire operation. He has a shave and teaches himself to speak in sentences and he and Sparko are seen at all the classiest joints with such dudes as Little Bob, Paul the Spook, Baby-Face Richardson and other sophisticates.

The Brain is beginning to enjoy things more than somewhat when certain disturbing facts come to his attention regarding bars which are providing a level of service not sanctioned by statute. In fact it is possible in these places to obtain a drink and a friendly conversation with a dame whose shirt keeps falling off, a few race results for the following Saturday, a bath or maybe just a wash or even part of a wash, and a little powder to keep household germs out of the nose.

These practices are greatly distressing to The Brain and he mentions his concern to a cop called Trousers O'Toole.

'It is a serious problem,' says Trousers O'Toole. 'And we are keen to apprehend those responsible.'

'Do you make any arrests in this regard?' asks The Brain.

'I put the sleeve on a very big suspect at one time but unfortunately someone falls through a manhole and flattens him before we can get him to court,' says Trousers O'Toole.

'Does anyone witness these events?' asks The Brain.

'Sparko and Huge Fat both attend the Police Ball at the time of the accident,' says Trousers O'Toole, 'but they are able to supply the name of the guy who perpetrates this outrage. We do not intend to take action, however, as the party concerned is very understanding about cops running bath-houses in their spare time.'

I am sitting in the buffet car of a train the other night playing a little three-spot with a character called Dreamtime and we shoot the breeze more than somewhat as we do not see each other since the year Dempsey hangs up his mittens.

In fact the last time I spot Dreamtime is when we scamper about after cattle during the days when there is still an honest living in moving the big herds from place to place, which is done at high speed in trucks and is most tiring and exhausting in every way. Unfortunately business falls off somewhat when a number of prominent animal-lovers are nabbed with the wrong cows and placed in the sneezer, which is a great injustice as it is very easy to make a mistake in the dark on unfamiliar property. I wish to state that Dreamtime and I know nothing of such mishaps and we take very little interest in cattle as a general proposition but a safe blows up in the office of a prominent banker at a time when I am in the bank sheltering from the rain and Dreamtime is outside sheltering in the car with the engine running.

We rattle along through the hinterland although of course we pay no attention to any natural wonders as our minds are on higher things. I do not think I ever see anyone to touch Dreamtime when it comes to three-spot or pontoon or even tossing aces into a hat and he relieves me of many potatoes. Many citizens consider it almost magical how many straights he obtains even with an unmarked deck, although personally I never see such a thing as an unmarked deck and Dreamtime winks whenever he hears one mentioned.

It seems Dreamtime is travelling to see his Great-Uncle who has some land left to him by a number of very ancient parties who throw a seven quite some time ago. And this land is not much use to anyone as it is somewhat barren and nothing grows on it as a result of the sun banging down and giving Mr and Mrs Plant a very tough time indeed. There is therefore some surprise when Dreamtime's Great-Uncle is sitting under a tree one day and two dudes arrive and offer to buy the place. This idea has very limited appeal for Dreamtime's Great-Uncle since he already has everything he wants in the way of a nice water-hole and a tree to sit under and is by no means interested in a retirement village of the type outlined in the proposal. I can see that Dreamtime is greatly concerned about these matters

'Our word is our bond,' says Button the Bantam.

as he commences dealing from the top of the deck and I manage to retrieve some of my potatoes.

At this point who should come strolling through from the next carriage but Little Bob and a citizen called Button the Bantam who is prominent in such things as protection. They sit down next to us, although there is plenty of room elsewhere as the carriage empties rapidly upon their arrival. Naturally we are very pleased to see such important figures and we smile very broadly in all directions.

Little Bob then states as follows: 'Hello, Dreamtime. This is a very big coincidence as we are just talking about you. We have a business proposition and we seek your involvement very keenly.'

'Our word is our bond,' says Button the Bantam.

'Uranium,' continues Little Bob. 'We locate an area which is practically made of the stuff and we are anxious to dig it up as it is worth billions.'

'Billions,' says Button the Bantam. 'Do you grasp the logical thrust of our bold initiative?'

'Where is this item located?' asks Dreamtime.

"It is under the ground at your Great-Uncle's very attractive premises,' says Little Bob, 'although we obtain no response from him to our generous offer which is excellent and unrepeatable and must close Friday.'

Button the Bantam then pulls out a deed giving Dreamtime a 49% shareholding in the Uranium Mine and slides it under his snorer for immediate consideration.

'I do not wish 49% if you wish 51%,' says Dreamtime. 'I affix my moniker only if we have 49% each and invite a third party to hold the remaining 2%.'

'This is extremely fair,' says Button the Bantam and he says to me like this, 'You hereby own 2% of this exciting venture.'

I am now in a very difficult position and of all the squeaks Dreamtime ever gets me in, this is the most dangerous. I look at Little Bob and he winks at me. Then I look at Button the Bantam who looks very confident and he winks at me too. I don't look at Dreamtime for more than half a second and I hardly move my head at all but he tells me later he never sees a more obvious wink in his life.

I am holding up a wall in Charley's little Speakeasy one evening around the time Cinderella loses her deposit, when I hear the sound of laughter coming from the kitchen. In fact it seems someone tells a very good joke indeed as this laughter is somewhat immoderate and contains a great deal of helpless shrieking and many huge roars.

Naturally I am drawn to the prospect of such entertainment as things are a little thin around this time and there is nothing like a spot of helpless shrieking or some huge roars to cheer the soul under such circumstances. So I slip into the kitchen and what I observe is most interesting in every respect, for a number of citizens including Paul the Spook, Baby-Face Richardson and Little Bob, are rolling about on the deck clutching their sides and crying for air. Furthermore a very prominent person named Easter Island, who has no sense of humour at all, is baying like a wolf and holding on to his trousers. Also among those present is a Cleaner called Nifty who tries to stand up but is laughing so much and slapping his thigh with such a high degree of appreciation that he tumbles into a sideboard, surprising a number of plates and saucers.

I am later told by Charley that the cause of these humorous events is an approach Little Bob receives from citizens representing the Queen of England. It seems the Windsors wish to appoint a new bagman for this region. Little Bob is wised-up as to the requirements and duties attaching to same and he listens with very great politeness and then appoints the Ipswich Kid. This is considered very hilarious although personally I can take or leave it as far as jokes go, but I see the difficulty as the Ipswich Kid is greatly opposed to the Windsors and their bagmen since the days of Hit the Turps.

Hit the Turps is very abstemious until he is about five years old but after that he opens the throttle somewhat and is frequently seen flying in formation at official functions. The Ipswich Kid is mobbed up with a party called the Great Man in those days and although the Great Man is widely respected by one and all, he is greatly despised by the authorities.

In fact the authorities become so distressed by the Great Man that they engage Easter Island to pop him in a sack at the earliest available and just in case this doesn't work they hire Hit the Turps to fire a number of shots into him and they provide

Furthermore a very prominent person named Easter
Island, who has no sense of humour at all, is baying
like a wolf and holding on to his trousers.

Hit the Turps with a Roscoe and they load it and point it at the Great Man and they show Hit the Turps the trigger and they show him his finger and they state as follows: 'Pull!'

As a result things are run for a bit by Easter Island and some guys with no tops to their heads but the citizens tire of this very easily and wish to see the Ipswich Kid take the whole operation over as he is considered slightly brighter. Who should step from the shadows at this point looking flushed and quietly confident but Little Bob who engages the Ipswich Kid in light conversation and pops some slugs into his back.

These events slow the Ipswich Kid down no little and a number of his very good friends take the opportunity to cover the matter up and help Little Bob get his hair right for the cameras. Such dudes as Slowly Slowly Bowen and Button the Bantam are notable for their contributions in this respect and the Ipswich Kid never forgets a face.

So when he hears that Little Bob wishes him to be the Windsors' bagman, he recalls Hit the Turps and Easter Island and how greatly opposed he is to Little Bob and the Windsors and to Easter Island and to bagmen generally and he goes for a walk to think about it.

I am passing the back of Mindy's at around 4 bells when I hear someone laughing and as I enter the premises I run into the Ipswich Kid and it seems he hears a very good one indeed as he has tears running down his pan and a large twinkle in his eye. When I seek information as to the nature of the joke he tells me he is by no means in favour of the idea of the Windsors' bagman removing citizens from their proper position as is the case with Hit the Turps and the Great Man. It is deeply disturbing to him that Little Bob can be placed in a sack by the Windsors' bagman and dropped over the side of a ship.

'I am against such a proposition on principle,' he says.

'What do you do?' I ask.

'I accept,' says the Ipswich Kid.

A TRIUMPH FOR LANDSLIDE HOWARD

Whenever there is only a thin crowd in Mindy's and such citizens as scribes and horse-players and other imposters obtain seats up near the bar, it is considered a very big shoo-in that something of great importance is happening somewhere else. In fact the cops who are always very worried by the number of prominent identities they find in Mindy's, are even more concerned when all they find is scribes and horse-players and other small-fry who do not know if their britches are on fire.

As a result when certain uniformed artisans come strolling through Mindy's one night along about eleven bells looking for someone to pop the old blue sleeve on, they are somewhat disturbed to observe nothing more dangerous than an old party named Cutsnake whose real moniker is Tuckey and who assures everyone he is a very murderous character although the only time Cutsnake ever gets in a fight he sneaks up and belts himself just under the ear with a crowbar.

I am sitting near the window sliding into a nice bowl of Mindy's excellent soup, whose virtues are numerous, when I become aware that Mindy is beckoning at me through the window so I pocket the bread-roll and join him. 'What occurs?' I ask.

'We're going to the big meeting,' he says, although I wish to say that I do not hear of any meeting until this time.

We wander a few yards to the east and then some yards to the south followed by some more yards to the east where we happen upon a little joint called Jimmy White's. I do not check my coat in since I figure the cops might arrive and rapid egress may be required and also I do not wish the bell-hop to get down on the bread-roll.

When we get inside, Mindy and I settle in near the stairs with a smiley old guy called Wing Ha who deals them off the arm in Jimmy White's for as long as anyone can remember. I take a peek about the place and realise that among those present are some of the hottest dudes in the world. In fact if the authorities get word that this gathering takes place they could dispatch the gendarmes and clean the whole country up more than somewhat.

In one corner is Little Bob who cools the Ipswich Kid off one night when the Ipswich Kid is facing the other way. Paul the Spook is with Button the Bantam who is on the lam over

134

'We are being over-run by Chinamen.'

a misunderstanding involving motor vehicles and next to them is Baby-Face Richardson who boffs a number of citizens on the blooter and claims to be interested in trees which is considered a good joke by one and all and very humorous in every respect. Slowly Slowly Bowen and Brainbox Jones shoot the breeze with Complete Dawkins, who operates a little protection concern among students and runs the potatoes over to Paul the Spook.

Suddenly everything becomes somewhat boisterous at the far end of the room and who should leap up on the table and haul out a big Roscoe but Landslide Howard who is most agitated and has a very wild look on his pan and who states as follows:

'We are being overrun by Chinamen.'

Naturally this proposition is met with some relief from those in attendance as the bootlegging of liquor and the placement of gambling transactions are not likely to disappear as a result of Chinamen, although Wing Ha shuffles about no little at this point and Mindy slips him the bread-roll.

'These Chinamen must be stopped,' continues Landslide. 'We must stop the Chinamen. The biggest single danger we confront in this society is Chinamen.'

Then he spots Wing Ha and commences to get very excited indeed and he says like this, 'There's one there! There's a Chinaman in Jimmy White's,' and he wishes to know if nothing is sacred.

'Get the owner,' shouts Landslide. 'Have the Chinaman thrown out. He has no place here. It's not natural.'

At this point Mindy moves forward slightly and remarks, 'He's with me. His name is Wing Ha and he works for me at one time and he is most dependable and what you state is a great deal of tripe.'

'You are a very big sap, Mindy,' states Landslide. 'Let us get the owner and see what occurs,' and they send for Jimmy White.

Well I see many dudes laugh in my time but I wish to say I never see anything to touch the way Mindy laughs when Landslide calls for Jimmy White and I ask him what causes this high degree of amusement.

'Jimmy White is not available just at the moment,' states Mindy, 'as a result of being dead since 1923. The owner of Jimmy White's is by no means Jimmy White but Wing Ha.'

One night I am taking the air along one of the major boulevards and I wish to say the air at this time of year is quite something as a result of a timely visit from old Mr Spring, who is very big as to such propositions as colour and trees becoming loaded with large helpings of blossom. Furthermore a number of yellow daffodils stick their beezers up out of the ground and wave about as if they just back the milkman's horse and it gets up and wins the Kentucky Derby.

I am having a lean on the side of an old Bakery when who should alight from a car but a character called the Dung Beetle, although when he alights the car is moving very briskly indeed and he alights through the window. In fact he alights with such speed that he hits the deck and slides about no little on his pan before he is able to slow down by hitting the old Bakery I mention earlier.

Naturally I draw no attention to the role played by the car and the window in his arrival and he himself seems somewhat anxious to play down the role of the Bakery as he picks himself up and wishes to know how I am and whether or not I can recall a springtime so rich in the bounty of nature. I recall that I do not see so many flowers about the place since the Firpo fight and he knocks the dust off his hat and states as follows: 'It is a profusion,' he says. 'The entire purlieu is festooned with jewels for the senses. I wonder do you have a John Roscoe as I wish to call upon Landslide Howard at the earliest convenience and pop a number of slugs into his pimple.'

Of course I do not carry a heater under any circumstances as they are greatly frowned upon by one and all and are even considered somewhat illegal. And if I find one in my coat pocket by mistake I am by no means likely to reveal the presence of same to a guy like the Dung Bettle as he is apt to get the wrong idea, and I do not wish guys getting the wrong idea, especially if they mean to pop slugs into other guys' pimples.

In fact I do not desire to converse further with the Dung Beetle, but he locates a C note somewhere in his tweeds and before I know it we are sitting down to a bowl of goulash in a little up-market trap in the same block and he tells me his story.

It seems the Dung Beetle's real moniker is Stone and he operates the big Counting House at one time when such activities

'It is difficult to hear him,' says the Dung Beetle,
'since he has a sheet over his pimple.'

are controlled by Landslide Howard and other prominent operators. This arrangement proceeds nicely until Landslide is boffed on the snorer one night by Little Bob and the Dung Beetle is nabbed by Paul the Spook and placed in a sack. Naturally the Dung Beetle is very much opposed to being placed in sacks and he always says if ever he gets Paul the Spook to himself vengeance is likely to be swift and terrible, although when he follows Paul the Spook one night with said vengeance in mind Paul the Spook stands in a shadow until the Dung Beetle happens along and then lands several good ones before placing him in another sack.

As a result of these events the Dung Beetle decides to stay on his own patch and direct his vengeance towards Landslide Howard who never hides in shadows, never lands any good ones and is lucky to get home without hurting himself. So the next time Landslide warns the citizens about the dangers of Chinamen, the Dung Beetle states as follows: 'What Landslide says is true in every particular and full of verisimilitude. All parties who hate Chinamen should gather behind Landslide.'

At this point Landslide becomes slightly concerned and greatly regrets opening his whistler on the matter and wishes he is never involved. In fact I understand he is secretly somewhat confused about Chinamen since he reads somewhere that they are people. But the Dung Beetle whips things up and arouses keen interest from a number of citizens who retain their privacy by wearing sheets over their pimples and conducting their AGM in a graveyard by the light of a burning crucifix. These developments trouble Landslide so greatly that he hauls out the old persuader and runs the Dung Beetle out of town.

'Is this why you wish to cool him off?' I ask. 'Or is it because he neglects to slow down while you alight from his offside window?'

'Oh no,' says the Dung Beetle. 'That is by no means the problem. What concerns me is that when I call upon him this evening I have a feeling he lectures me about the dangers of my approach.'

'You are not certain?' I ask.

'It is difficult to hear him,' says the Dung Beetle, 'since he has a sheet over his pimple.'

A COMPLETE CHRISTMAS

I am stepping out along a well-lit thoroughfare one evening thinking evil thoughts about an old boiler who is given to me as a sure thing in the 3.15 but who is lucky to finish ahead of the winner of the 4.35, when I notice a commercial transaction taking place in the doorway of a book store. A number of citizens empty their pockets and hand their potatoes to a little dude with a hat pulled down over his eyes and in return the dude prevents his Roscoe from discharging into their noggins.

When I get close enough I observe that this dude is none other than Complete Dawkins and I immediately assume the citizens wish to purchase an education as Complete Dawkins is very prominent in this line, although there is some talk that Complete's activities cause many students to toss the towel in and take up other trades, such as break-ins and a little bank work and one thing and another.

Personally I think he carves out just the right section of the market since students are greatly interested in ideas and the idea of not receiving a pellet in the swede has great appeal through the ages.

Complete is somewhat distinctive as to appearance. He wears a beard and looks like the sort of guy the cops are always seeking with regard to various matters, although the cops give up seeking any information from Complete some time ago as he is somewhat difficult to pin down on details, such as what actually occurs. In fact if Complete says it is a nice day it is considered wise to pack a raincoat and possibly some snow-shoes and maybe an ice-pick.

Naturally I do not mention these thoughts socially and furthermore I do not make with any hellos when I spot him as I do not wish to be seen making hellos with such a character as Complete Dawkins under any circumstances.

Unfortunately he steps in beside me and nothing will do but we must have Christmas drinks. So the next thing I know I am in an up market trap called The Club being approached by a gorilla in a tux who wishes to know our pleasure and informs me it is by no means unusual to wear socks.

Complete seems to order more Christmas drinks than somewhat and what with this and that I am standing beside a big piano with Button the Bantam at around two bells doing the high bits in 'Silent Night' although of course we are obliged

Complete insists that Little Bob must receive his
gift by 5 o'clock.

to shout no little on account of the noise. Complete then states that he must arrange a Christmas present for Little Bob and slips into a corner with Paul the Spook who is apparently a very big expert on such matters.

I wish to say that practically everyone attends Christmas drinks at The Club and if I am not full of good cheer I am likely to be greatly concerned about some of the prominent identities among those present. There is Little Bob and Baby-Face Richardson and a very amusing character called Flagfall Rae who has a bib on and gives a bucket of oysters a terrible hiding. Then there is Paul the Spook who buys Slowly Slowly Bowen a Christmas drink and shares a joke with him. They seem to get along extremely well and I make a mental note to obtain plenty of 11 to 5 on Slowly Slowly Bowen being popped in a sack very soon indeed.

It is around 4 when Complete hauls out a big red and white fluffy suit and states that he wishes me to be Santa. Of course I have no desire to be Santa as right at the moment I am fully stretched being me, but I can see that many citizens may cease to believe in Santa if they spot Complete's pan inside the fancy costume. He gives me a bag of presents which are most festive and colourful in every way and I am especially taken with Little Bob's as it is the only one that ticks loudly.

Complete insists that Little Bob must receive his gift by 5 o'clock or maybe 6 at the very latest, but when I throw it back in the bag Complete hits the deck and pulls his hands up over his pimple. It is because of these worrying developments that as soon as Complete departs I place Little Bob's present behind a potted plant in the lift and make sure Santa is all finished and in another part of town by daylight.

Naturally I am greatly surprised to learn of the large explosion which occurs at The Club around dawn as apparently the building is replaced by a very deep hole. From what I read in the bladders there is no one in the joint at the time, although a cop I run into in Mindy's states that this is by no means the case.

'Do you not hear about Complete Dawkins?' he asks. 'We receive a phone-call from him just before the explosion.'

'Does he alert you to impending events?' I ask.

'No,' says the cop. 'He calls to say he is stuck in the lift.'